D0375149

GRIEVING *the* LOSS *of a* LOVED ONE

Also by Kathe Wunnenberg

Grieving the Child I Never Knew

Longing for a Child

Kathe Wunnenberg

Grieving *the* Loss *of a* Loved One

A DEVOTIONAL COMPANION

ZONDERVAN®

ZONDERVAN.com/
AUTHORTRACKER
follow your favorite authors

ZONDERVAN

Grieving the Loss of a Loved One
Copyright © 2000 by Kathe Wunnenberg

Requests for information should be addressed to:
Zondervan, *Grand Rapids, Michigan 49530*

ISBN 978-0-310-22778-6

Interior design: Laura Klynstra Blost

Printed in the United States of America

09 10 11 12 13 14 15 • 32 31 30 29 28 27 26 25 24 23 22 21 20 19 18 17 16 15 14

With love and gratitude to my husband, Rich Wunnenberg.
You inspired me through your own grief journey to trust God.
Thank you for being my life partner, best friend, encourager,
a shoulder I could cry on, and a candle to light my darkest
moments. You are a true reflection of Christ to me.

And to all those who are journeying through their own grief.
You keep me motivated to press on in spite of my pain.

CONTENTS

ACKNOWLEDGMENTS

WRITING A BOOK IS a lot like trying to have a baby. It may happen easily or never, or it may take years. While this project came together, I was in the process of grieving the loss of my son and recovering from two miscarriages. I was on a physical, emotional, and spiritual roller coaster. I didn't know if I would have the endurance or stamina to deliver the project.

Then I discovered I was pregnant again. I panicked. I felt I didn't need more illustrations about loss. I had to trust God and not lean on my own understanding. As my waistline disappeared and my deadline approached, my fax machine, e-mail, phone, and mailbox became flooded with insights from people who had lost loved ones. They affirmed the need for this book. They gave me the courage to labor on and to stay focused on the outcome of changing lives.

This project has enlarged my soul and stretched me beyond my limits. It has unleashed my passion to provide hope to the hurting and to proclaim the good news of God's faithfulness. I am amazed as I bend over my six-month bulging belly to look at my completed manuscript, ready to be delivered into my editor's hands. It has been a long and intense labor of love that I could have never completed without the support of many people. May this "baby" produce fruit and multiply God's kingdom. I salute my "co-laborers":

The Zondervan Publishing Team

Thank you for believing in me and seeing the potential in this project. I deeply appreciate your creative staff, commitment to excellence, encouragement, and prayers.

Ann Spangler, you're a great senior acquisitions editor and encourager! You see beyond conception. Your ability, flexibility, and sensitivity made it a less painful labor.

Janet Kobobel Grant, you're a great editing coach who helped me to breathe to the finish! Thanks for your insights and heart for this project.

Verlyn Verbrugge, thanks for your finishing touches.

The Contributors

Thanks to those who provided me with valuable feedback from my questionnaire and with personal insights and stories about your losses. I received many moving stories but could share only a portion of them in this book.

Thanks to my mom, Alice Stephens, for keeping the faxes coming with research, ideas, and verses. Thanks, Mom, for your love and prayers and for being my biggest cheerleader through the years.

The PIT Team (Personal Intercessory Team)

Thanks to forty-six of you throughout the United States and Canada for laboring on your knees for this project and me. You helped carry me through to completion! I hope you'll continue through the next book. If I had to choose between Pitosin and prayer, prayer delivers!

The Mentors

Thanks to John McAdam, who instilled the dream to write; the University of Missouri's journalism school, which sharpened my skill; Carol Kent, who saw my potential as a Christian communicator, cheered me on, and published my story in her book; Judy Couchman, for modeling perseverance as a writer, for teaching me, and for connecting me with Ann Spangler; Traci Mullins, for reading my proposal; The Vision Group, for coming alongside me with support and encouragement; Dottie Escabedo-Frank and Margie Erbe, for being my grief mentors.

The Up-Close-and-Personal Local Team

Rich Wunnenberg, my husband, best friend, technical support, encourager, and grief mentor, thank you for helping me to fulfill my dream of "being pregnant and writing a book" and for sharing the labor with me by listening to me read every story aloud.

Jake Wunnenberg, you're a terrific son, who is sensitive to my needs and gives great hugs! Thanks for sharing picnics at the cemetery and happy-sad tears with me.

Lisa Jernigan and Jan James for being Jesus-with-skin-on friends, who walked with me through the fire of my losses. Thanks for loving me unconditionally and just being there.

Christian Business Women's Association for reflecting Christ to me.

Mountain Park Community Church for your meals and love in action.

Jesus Christ, You are the great physician and true deliverer of this project. Nothing is impossible with You. Thanks for being my Lord and Savior.

Reading for Special Days or Needs

SPECIAL OCCASIONS, HOLIDAYS, AND personal circumstances may trigger your grief and expose a new dimension of living life without your loved one. When you encounter these times in your journey and desire encouragement or a fresh perspective, turn to the selected reading for that specific day or need.

Your Journey Through Grief

LOSING SOMEONE YOU LOVE through death is painful and personal. You soon learn that grief can't be confined to a method, time frame, or event; it's a process. Grief is an unpredictable, solitary, and unforgettable experience, one that can't be healed in a moment, a month, or even a lifetime. Grief ebbs and flows, like the swelling waves of an ocean. One moment we feel engulfed by a wave of sorrow. The next we are lifted by waves of hope and acceptance. Grief is an irregular tide that often takes us by surprise.

How you respond to it determines the quality and direction of your life. You can choose to allow it to drown you emotionally, or you can allow loss to enlarge your soul. As difficult as it is to lose a loved one, grief can deepen you as a person and increase your empathy and your trust in God. Loss can open your eyes to see the same world from a different viewpoint . . . with new scenery. In that sense, grief is a journey.

Whether you've recently suffered loss and are beginning your grief journey, are several years into your journey, or are somewhere in between, a void will always exist in your life from losing your loved one. Each season of your life may find you blazing a new trail as you discover a different dimension of your loss. And just when you think your journey through grief has finally ended, you see a fork in the road and find yourself trudging down a familiar path that you've walked before.

Grieving the Loss of a Loved One gives you permission to be who you are and where you are in your journey. Take a moment to glance at the table of contents. You may want to use it as your compass, helping you to find the section of the book that best fits your need each day. Or you may want to read the book straight through, one devotional per day. However you use the book, let it help you wherever you are on the journey.

If you need to cry, weep with all your heart.

If you need to vent, tell God the whole truth about how you're feeling.

If you're ready to celebrate, do it with gusto.

My hope is that you will adopt *Grieving the Loss of a Loved One* as a personal companion. Think of it as a good friend with whom you can share laughs, tears, dreams, and your innermost thoughts. Whether you read this devotional guide daily or as the need arises, highlight it, dog-ear it, write in it. My prayer is that it will be a tool to guide you to a deeper understanding of who God is.

I pray the stories that follow will comfort your soul and give you courage to press on in your journey. What I have written has grown out of my personal experience of losing my infant son and three children through miscarriages; being married to a man who lost both of his parents as a child; and encountering life losses through my parents' divorce, cross-country moves, infertility, adoption, and career transitions.

I believe that God, who suffered the loss of His only Son, understands our worst pain and our darkest thoughts. Wherever you are on the journey through grief, God wants not only to speak to you but also to draw near. I hope the stories, Scripture, prayers, and the opportunity to record your own thoughts, questions, and prayers in the journal section will help to bring healing and a closer relationship with the one who loves you.

I am convinced that we sometimes go through difficult experiences so we can encourage others who will later endure similar hardships. As a matter of fact, this book wouldn't have been possible without the men, women, and children who shared their personal insights and stories. I have written this book not as an expert, not as someone who has arrived, but as a fellow griever, still on the journey. Behind the pages of *Grieving the Loss of a Loved One* is a person who can relate to at least some of what you are experiencing. And behind that person is a faithful God.

YOUR JOURNEY
THROUGH DENIAL

Denying: *to declare untrue, to disclaim connection with or responsibility for, to refuse to accept.*

God never comes through the door that I hold open for
    Him,
But always knocks at the one place which I have walled
    up with concrete.
But if I do not let Him in there,
He turns away altogether.

HELMUT THIELICKE

It's a funny thing about grief — handling it efficiently
doesn't make it go away.

AUTHOR UNKNOWN

How do I manage a difficulty? Well, at first I try to
walk past it. If that does not help, I try to climb over it;
and when I cannot climb over it, to crawl underneath.
And when that is not possible, I go straight through —
God and me.

CORRIE TEN BOOM
CLIPPINGS FROM MY NOTEBOOK

JOURNEY THROUGH THE FOG TO REALITY

■ ■ ■

You can't heal a wound by saying it's not there!

JEREMIAH 6:14, TLB

Shock.

Disbelief.

Numbness.

Confusion.

YOU MAY ENCOUNTER SOME of these feelings when facing the reality of your loss. At times you may feel as if you're walking on a road through a dense fog, stumbling through the nothingness that surrounds you, groping for an escape yet finding none.

Getting fogged in was a common occurrence when we lived in Oregon. Most mornings I would peer out our family room window expecting to see fir trees and mountains, only to find they had vanished once again.

Whenever the fog rolled in, I felt out of control, thinking about airport delays and white-knuckle driving. Over time, though, I learned to cope with the eerie white vapor and to forge through it — sometimes with the help of my car's high beams. I realized the impairment was temporary, and that gave me hope to endure. By afternoon the fog would lift, and I could see clearly again.

That's how it is with grief. Our initial shock over a loved one's death may cause us to deny it or ignore it. We may feel lost, paralyzed, in limbo, somewhere between reality and a dream.

This can't be happening! you think.

But it is.

I don't want to face it!

But you have to.

Maybe not right this moment. That's okay. But if you want to journey through grief, you must look beyond the clouds created by denial and fears. With God's strength and in His timing, the fog will begin to clear, and you'll be able to see reality again. It may not be what you want to see, and it may look quite different than before, but it is a necessary part of your journey through grief.

How are you coping with your loss? When you look out the window of your circumstance today, what do you see? Are you in the fog, denying reality? Or is the fog beginning to clear to reveal a new landscape?

> *Lord, it's so hard to cope with what has happened. I don't want to believe my loved one is gone. I keep hoping I'll wake up and discover this is only a dream. I feel so unsure about where I am right now. I can't see what life should look like. Please help me through this part of the journey. You say that You will never leave me or forsake me and that You will be a lamp to my feet. Please be my headlights and lead me through this time of uncertainty and pain. Amen.*

MY PERSONAL JOURNEY

My Personal Journey

OUT OF THE GRAY ZONE

■ ■ ■

*For you were once darkness, but now you are light in the Lord. Live as chil-
dren of light (for the fruit of the light consists in all goodness, righteousness
and truth).*

EPHESIANS 5:8—9

HAVE YOU EVER TRIED to ignore the truth only to discover that it keeps
popping up anyway?

In my mid-twenties my hair started to change colors. People would
stop me to ask, "Who frosts your hair?" I couldn't bring myself to diffuse their compliments by telling them my silvery strands were natural.

Conversely, no one has ever stopped me to ask, "How did you get
your wrinkles?" I'm glad they ignore those truths. When I look in the
mirror, I can't deny the truth that I'm getting older, that I'm not the same
person I used to be.

My hairdresser finally convinced me I couldn't ignore the aging
process and keep hoping my gray would go away. She helped me face
the truth that I would look better by either going gray all the way or covering it up. Although I was content with either choice, I decided to be
adventurous for my fortieth birthday, and I colored my hair. Amazingly,
facing the truth about aging and making adjustments to it rather than
denying it set me free and gave me a better look. Now when people stop
me to ask about my hair, I proclaim, "I'm out of the gray zone of denial,
I'm coloring my hair!"

Whether it's wrinkles, aging, hair color, or the loss of a loved one, ignoring the truth leads to the gray zone of denial. Loss is painful. Some days, as we journey through grief, we look around and wonder what is true and what is false. Did this really happen? Am I dreaming?

Things may appear to be the same. We may even try to ignore the truth of our loss by keeping our loved one's clothes in the closet and the bedroom the same. We go through the motions and deny that our loved one is really gone. When others stop us to comment about how great we look and how well we're coping, we nod and smile. We don't want to diffuse their compliment and tell them that we're covering up our grief. And we're relieved they don't notice the strands of hurt plaited through our life. But we look in the mirror and see the pain in our eyes. We're not the same person we used to be.

As we journey through the grief, God may gently help us face the truth of our loss. Then we have a choice to make: to face the truth and make adjustments in our life or to continue to ignore it. Denying our pain and disappointment only leads to more hurt. Facing the truth sets us free and allows us to move on in our journey through grief.

God understands the gray zone of denial and can help us face the truth. When Jesus told Peter that he would deny Him three times before the rooster crowed, Peter refused to believe it. He wouldn't deny his Lord. Yet, he did. Stressed, pressured, alone, and afraid, he pretended he didn't know Jesus when others confronted him.

Peter's grief over his denial must have been overwhelming. He wasn't the same person he used to be. Only the truth could set him free. That's why Jesus gently helped Peter to face the truth and make adjustments, forgave him, and gave him a new look as "The Rock."

Are you tired of covering up the pain of your loss? Maybe it's time to move out of the gray zone of denial and let God's truth set you free. Your loss has changed you. The start of your new look could be just a prayer away.

Precious Lord, I've been ignoring my pain and going through the motions. Help set me free. Be the Truth in my life and expose hidden strands of hurt and disappointment. I know I'm not the same person I used to be. Help me to embrace my new identity apart from my loved one. Transform my gray of grief into a new look that lets the truth of my loss and my potential in You shine through. Amen.

My Personal Journey

_____

_____

_____

_____

_____

_____

_____

_____

_____

_____

_____

_____

_____

GRIEF MIRAGE

■ ■ ■

*If anyone is thirsty, let him come to me and drink, For the Scriptures declare
that rivers of living water shall flow from the inmost being of anyone who
believes in me.*

JOHN 7:37B—38, TLB

A SCENE IN AN old Western movie depicts a cowboy stranded in the
desert without a horse. An ocean of sand surrounds him. The sun blazes
down. His mouth is parched and dry. His canteen is empty. His only
hope for survival is to find shelter and water. He stumbles up a hill and
peers down into the valley. He can't believe his eyes. In the distance is
an oasis with trees and water. With renewed hope he rushes toward it
and bends down to scoop up the water in his hands. He starts to drink
it . . . then chokes. He spits out a mouthful of sand.

Anyone suffering from extreme thirst or mental or physical strain can
experience a phenomenon known as a mirage. It can even happen when
we suffer the pain of grief.

After his wife Rachel died, I can only imagine how Jacob must have
felt being left alone to parent their two sons, Joseph and Benjamin. Did
he try to manage his home in the same way it was managed before, as if
nothing had ever happened? When he came home at night, was he
greeted by Rachel's embrace and the aroma of fresh cut flowers in her
hair? As he reached out to grab her hand to pray at dinner, could he feel
her warm, gentle touch? How his heart must have ached when he
tucked Joseph and Benjamin in at night and recalled her lullabies and

laughter. And every time he kissed them good-night, and they looked up at him with their big brown eyes, he saw Rachel staring back. Her penetrating eyes ignited the passion in Jacob's being. He closed his eyes in bed at night and could feel her heart beating next to his. When he awoke from his slumber he was confused. Was Rachel really gone or was it all a dream? This experience felt so real, Jacob was afraid others might think he was crazy.

Grief can play a key role in a mirage-like occurrence when we ignore the pain of our loss and refuse to allow ourselves to feel. Denial is a way for us to survive and cope, though we may not understand at the time what we are doing. Our journey through denial may affect each of us differently. Hearing or seeing imaginary things might not be your experience, but thinking that your loved one is going to call you any moment may be.

Sometimes our emotions play tricks on us and appear to be something they're not. Like the cowboy, we trudge through the heavy sand of our grief. The trek is lonely and the surroundings desolate, but we think we're in control and coping fine. Then we see an oasis in the distance. We run toward it and scoop up the sweet joy that awaits us . . . and we nearly choke. We spit out what we thought was reality only to discover it was really denial.

Our grief may cause us to have difficulty discerning reality. We may need to seek professional help or to talk to another person to gain perspective.

God understands where we are. When we run to Him, He is our true oasis. When we scoop up His living water, our thirst will be satisfied with the truth.

Maybe it's time for reality to come out, to talk to another person about the pain of your loss and to run to the One who will satisfy your thirst with truth. He is waiting. Run to Him.

God, I've been wandering in the desert of denial trying to survive the pain of my loss. I'm parched and dry. I'm thirsty for the truth. My mind and emotions play tricks on me. I don't want to live a mirage. Show me whom I can talk to today who will help me cope. Forgive me for not running to You sooner. Here I am. Quench my thirst with the living water of Your Word today. Amen.

❧

MY PERSONAL JOURNEY

_____

_____

_____

_____

_____

_____

_____

_____

_____

_____

_____

_____

_____

_____

_____

_____

SAILING TO THE ICEBERG OF DENIAL

You will know the truth, and the truth will set you free.

JOHN 8:32

ON APRIL 10, 1912, the whole world was talking about an amazing new ship, the Titanic, which was about to set sail from England to America. Newspapers called it "The Wonder Ship" and "The Rich Man's Special." Like a floating palace, the ship was nearly four city blocks long and as tall as an eleven-story building. Experts agreed she was the safest ship ever.

Crowds lined the shore. Flags snapped in the breeze. Music filled the air. Passengers waved good-bye to their friends. The engines roared and the ship steamed out of the harbor. The Titanic had begun its first voyage. No one ever dreamed this would also be its last.

Two days later the Titanic was in icy waters off the coast of Canada. Since it was late at night, most of the passengers were asleep. Suddenly the lookout saw a dark shape and sounded the alarm, "Iceberg straight ahead!" But the seaman steering the ship couldn't divert the Titanic quickly enough, and the giant iceberg scraped along the side of the ship. There didn't appear to be much damage. Most passengers were unaware anything had even happened. Yet, the terrible truth was the massive iceberg, beneath the water's surface where no one could see, had severely damaged the ship.

During our grief journey we may look as if we're coping with our loss. We may even start to believe that it hasn't deeply affected us and that we're unsinkable. We keep sailing through life with a smile on our face. Friends and family close to us ask us how we're really doing and whether we're denying the intensity of our feelings. Others who have experienced the loss of a loved one may even warn us to be on the lookout for the iceberg of denial. But we ignore them and sail along. The darkness closes in, and then we see it: a massive mountain of feelings, and we're moving straight for it. "Iceberg of denial straight ahead!" We try to divert our life around it, but it's too late. The mound of hidden feelings beneath the surface cuts into us, and we start to sink as we face the reality of the pain of losing our loved one.

Then we learn the truth: We are not unsinkable, and we have ignored or avoided facing our loss. When we hit our iceberg of denial, we must plunge beneath the surface to examine hidden hurts. We are forced to face the damage. This is a necessary part of healing in our journey through grief, to face the truth. Unlike the Titanic, your iceberg will not sink you, but instead — as you take inventory of grief's damage — you can make the repairs that will allow you to stay afloat.

Facing the truth may be a process of discovery through the years. During some seasons you will think you're coping with your loss, during others you're not.

If you don't take an honest look at what's happening, you might crash into the iceberg of denial again. Instead, you can take safety measures to prevent that from happening often. Being truthful with yourself and others is a first step. The second step is to recognize that it's okay to feel the pain, even if it's a long time after your loss. Another safety measure is to be alert that denial does exist and that you may need a warning from God or others to help you face it. The truth may not remove your anguish, but it eventually will set you free and allow you to journey on.

God, I feel as if I'm doing okay since my loss. It hasn't affected me like I thought it would. Others are amazed at my response and how I appear to cope. Is this really the truth, or is denial hidden beneath the surface? Show me the truth today. Be my lookout and warn me as I sail through life. Prevent me from sinking. Rescue me with Your truth and help me to journey on. Amen.

My Personal Journey

TRUTH OR DENIAL?

∎ ∎ ∎

Send forth your light and your truth, let them guide me; let them bring me to your holy mountain, to the place where you dwell.

PSALM 43:3

TWO WOMEN ENTER A courtroom and stand in front of the king. One holds a baby; the other clings to an empty blanket. The woman with empty arms rushes forward and tells Solomon about her son's birth. She chokes back tears as she shares how the other woman gave birth to a son a few days later. But her baby died. This woman swapped the dead baby for the living baby while the new mother slept. "That's my baby," she moans.

Silence pervades the room. The king sees the pain in her eyes. He turns to face the woman holding the baby. She glares at him and shouts, "No, the living one is my son and the dead one is hers!"

What fear must have come into the heart of the real mother. What boldness and denial were yet in the heart of the mother whose child was dead.

Solomon commands an attendant to bring him a sword. "Divide the living child in two, and give half to the one and half to the other."

"Oh, my lord, give her the living child, and do not slay it," cries the woman with empty arms.

"Divide it!" says the other.

The truth cannot be denied. The king, who is the wisest of judges, knows by the two mothers' words who is the real mother.

I can imagine how grateful that woman was as she reached for her baby and held him once again in her arms. Her tears turned to smiles and the heaviness in her heart was replaced with joy.

But what about the other woman? Was she really cruel-hearted and vindictive, or was she a desperate, grieving mother who would do anything to have her son back?

I can only imagine the shock and pain she must have felt when she discovered her baby was dead. Did she convince herself that he was only sleeping and would wake up soon? How tormenting for her to hear the other baby's healthy cry. No one understood the anguish she felt. She couldn't face her loss. I wonder if she thought that just being near what she longed for would lessen her pain.

Clutching her lifeless baby, she tiptoed into the room where everyone was sleeping. She bent down and peeked at the tiny breathing bundle. This felt so familiar. *I'll pick him up and hold him just for a few minutes*, she thought. She gently laid her baby down and scooped up the living baby into her arms. She didn't remember how long she held him or what happened next. All she knew was joy returned to her heart and a sense of relief that the death was just a terrible nightmare.

I'm not justifying or condoning her actions; yet I can relate to her pain and understand how grief can drive us to do, think, or say strange things. My brother and his wife had a healthy baby boy just a few days before my son was born and died. Although I was excited for them, the first few times I saw my nephew, he reminded me of what I longed for but didn't have. Sometimes when I held him, I would imagine that this was my son and allowed myself to feel the joy of a new mother, even if only for a few moments.

Now, when I look at my nephew, I see my nephew, a bright, handsome boy who is a sweet reminder to me of the age my son would be. God used him in my journey through denial to fill my empty arms, comfort my grieving soul, and help me to face the reality of my loss.

Fantasizing that your loved one is still alive and will come walking through the door is one way to cope. Sometimes facing reality is too painful and denying your loss is a temporary way to survive. In the right time, God will help you to face reality and cope with your loss.

God, it feels like a dream that my loved one is gone and won't walk through the door to tell me this is a nightmare. My pain is too raw to face that reality right now. I want to pretend this never happened. It's like I'm standing in a courtroom with the truth on one side of me and denial on the other. You are the wise, discerning judge, and You see my pain and the truth. Help me cope with the truth. Reveal it to me today. Amen.

My Personal Journey

_____

_____

_____

_____

_____

_____

_____

_____

_____

_____

_____

_____

_____

My Personal Journey

YOUR JOURNEY
THROUGH VENTING

Venting: *to discharge, expel; to give expression to; to relieve pressure.*

■ ■ ■

All anger is not sinful, because some degree of it, and on some occasions, is inevitable. But it becomes sinful and contradicts the rule of Scripture when it is conceived upon slight and inadequate provocation, and when it continues long.

WILLIAM PALEY

Anger is really disappointed hope.

ERICA JONG

We can react with anger when we are hurt. We can strike out or use silence as a weapon to express our pain. Or we can release it by willingly forgiving others and ourselves.

KATHE WUNNENBERG

JOURNEY TO THE
VOLCANO OF ANGER

"In your anger do not sin": Do not let the sun go down while you are still angry.

EPHESIANS 4:26

ON MAY 18, 1980, in southwestern Washington, a volcano that had been dormant since 1857 erupted with such violence that the mountain's top was blown off, and a cloud of ash and gases soared to an altitude of twelve miles. As a result of the eruption, the mountain's elevation was decreased from 9,677 feet to 8,364 feet. The blast killed fifty-seven people and destroyed all life in an area the size of a large city.

When my husband and I moved to the northwest a few days after Mount St. Helen's erupted, we didn't expect any aftereffects, but ash showers were common. Gray dust sprinkled from the sky onto cars, homes, and streets. In some areas it poured down, requiring dump trucks to haul off the debris. People carried umbrellas and sported surgical masks as ash-shield attire.

Several months later we drove to see the mountain. What had once been acres of plants, flowers, and green trees was a vast, barren area, charred and cluttered with debris. A blanket of ashes covered the ground. The stench of putrid gases and burnt wood filled the air. Steam spewed from the disfigured mountain. We felt uneasy as we wondered, Could this happen again?

In our grief journey, sometimes our feelings remain dormant and inactive for weeks, months, or years. We don't realize they are building up until, without warning, something triggers them, and we blow! Our anger erupts and devastates everything and everyone in its path. The emotional blast shocks us and those around us.

Where did that come from? we wonder. Then we realize that our journey through grief has taken us to the volcano of anger.

Jerry remembers the day he blew. A year had passed since his wife's death, and he was planning to play golf with a friend. As he was dressing, he sensed uneasiness welling up within him. When his friend arrived early and urged him to hurry, without warning Jerry picked up his golf shoes and hurled them at the freshly painted family room wall. Then he slumped to the floor and wept. Where did that come from? he wondered.

To this day, Jerry still is not sure, but he's convinced that something triggered his hidden anger over his loss. He felt uneasy every time he looked at the aftereffects of his eruption—the black marks on his wall. He wondered if this would ever happen again.

Hidden anger can be devastating. Sooner or later, if we cork our feelings from our loss, we will blow. I'm in the process of learning to recognize the different faces of my emotions and their cause. Behind my face of disappointment and hurt are unmet expectations and others' insensitive comments or actions. I wear my face of fear when I feel uncertain, unable to trust, and anxious about change. When my anger flares, it's time to take inventory and expose the true face of my emotions.

I have a choice to make when I discover hidden emotions. Confront them, keep them current, and find peace, or continue to internalize my feelings, allow them to build, and eventually blow again. Reflecting on Jerry's eruption and the black marks on his wall reminds me that my eruptions can have lasting effects too.

Your grief journey may lead you to the volcano of anger. You may not even realize you are there until you erupt without warning. You may feel devastated, regretting what you said or did. But the good news is that God understands and is willing to transform the devastating ashes of your hidden grief into beauty. He will be your gauge, the One who puts the check in your spirit when you start to internalize your emotions and to allow them to build. His truth will gently remind you to keep your feelings current and not to let the sun go down on your anger. Trust Him with your hidden disappointments, hurts, and fears. Release them to Him today and let Him calm your building volcano of anger.

God, please forgive me for allowing my anger to erupt. I'm sorry if I hurt others. Be my gauge and let me know when I need to confront the different faces of my emotions and the underlying pain from my grief that triggers my anger. Don't let the sun go down on my anger today. Reveal to me my hidden disappointments, hurts, and fears. I release them to You right now. Calm my volcano of anger. Amen.

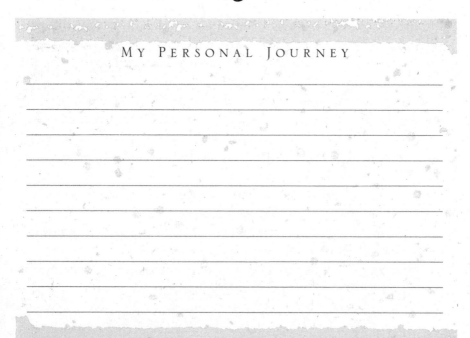

MY PERSONAL JOURNEY

JOURNEY FROM ENVY TO ADMIRATION

Who is wise and understanding among you? Let him show it by his good life, by deeds done in the humility that comes from wisdom. But if you harbor bitter envy and selfish ambition in your hearts, do not boast about it or deny the truth.

JAMES 3:13—14

ALTHOUGH THE BIBLE CALLS us to "mourn with those who mourn" and "rejoice with those who rejoice," sometimes in our journey through grief, it's hard to rejoice for others. If we're really honest, we might admit that we wish things were different and that we could trade places with certain people. We may discover that we avoid them and situations where they might be because it's too painful and triggers our emotions.

Our reaction to others may be unpredictable and may shock us at times. For example, when a friend asked me to hold her son during the worship service, reluctantly yet willingly I agreed. I felt numb and disconnected. I was afraid this simple act of holding a baby would trigger the hurt from my grief even though my son had been dead for more than a year. I was thrilled when I made it through the church service without breaking down. Little did I know that an earthquake had hit my emotions, and the aftershock would come soon.

Later that evening, I wasn't prepared for my explosive response. I snapped at my husband, slammed the door, and sped out of the driveway sobbing uncontrollably. I was shocked at my anger. It scared me.

As I reflected on the day's happenings, I began to think about the woman who had handed me her son. She had something I didn't. Her arms were full. Mine were empty. I longed to have a son too.

My envy had been exposed. I was allowing it to destroy my relationship with others and with the Lord. It was robbing me of the love and joy I was supposed to have for others, but it had been so camouflaged in my grief that I hadn't detected it until now. My envy had to go.

We can learn from Sarah, a fellow struggler. Sarah has more lines of print in the Bible than any other woman, is commended as a "holy woman of old," and is among God's Who's Who of faith. Wealthy, charming, and beautiful, she was Abraham's wife. God promised that she would be the mother of nations.

However, Sarah endured years of barrenness. Her pain must have multiplied every time she saw a newborn baby in another woman's arms. Running low on patience, Sarah went to extreme measures to obtain a child by arranging for a surrogate mother with her husband. But Sarah's temporary admiration for Hagar ignited into explosive envy, and the other woman and her son were banished.

This dilemma affected Sarah's faith and drove her back to God. Her grief and longing nourished the development of her relationship with God. Sarah stands as proof that God is trustworthy. She reminds us that although others will fail us, God will not. She challenges us to admire God and not envy others.

Like Sarah, we all have areas of our lives that don't meet our expectations. In our grief journey, we may be tempted to compare ourselves to others and long for what they have. The pain of our loss can distort how we think, feel, and respond.

Who has what you want? What triggers your reaction to them? How can you turn your envy of others into admiration for God?

God, it seems as though everywhere I look, others have what I want. They have their loved ones, and I don't. Sometimes I wish I could exchange places. It hurts when I'm around them and it triggers the emotions of my grieving soul. Help me not to compare myself to others. Please forgive me for my silent resentment and explosive outbursts. I'm sorry for hurting others. Fill the longing in my soul with Your comfort and self-control. Replace my envy of others with admiration for You. Amen.

MY PERSONAL JOURNEY

JOURNEY TO STILL WATER

■ ■ ■

Then they cried out to the LORD in their trouble, and he brought them out of
their distress. He stilled the storm to a whisper; the waves of the sea were hushed.
They were glad when it grew calm, and he guided them to their desired haven.

PSALM 107:28–30

ON THE FIRST DAY of summer vacation, Vicki, her son, Rew, and their
new puppy arrived at the lake to water-ski with friends. Although this
was only Rew's second time skiing, the ritual was a familiar one to Vicki.
She loved the water. Some of her favorite childhood memories involved
water, and she hoped to pass the legacy on to her son. Her eyes sparkled
as she gazed at her son sitting in the boat and she anticipated the memories they would make together.

They arrived in the secluded cove late in the afternoon. The water
was calm. The conditions were perfect for skiing. Everyone took turns
climbing in and out of the boat. Then Rew plopped into the water to ski.

Vicki watched her son emerge from the water and cling to the
towrope behind the boat puttering slowly through the cove. She was so
proud of Rew. Then, without warning, a sleek, high-powered speedboat
roared into the cove. Vicki watched in helpless horror as the boat struck
her son, and he disappeared beneath the water.

In that moment Vicki's life changed forever. She replayed that scene
in her mind while the divers searched for Rew. Seven days later they
recovered his body.

Vicki had already lost all the men in her life — her father, grandfathers, and uncles. She had even experienced the death of her marriage when her ex-husband left her for another woman. And now her son was gone and her anger flared.

"Why are You punishing me, God? I don't understand how You could allow this to happen!"

During the seven years that followed her son's death, Vicki turned her anger inward and simply refused to cry. She started drinking and indulged herself with periodic spending sprees. Masking her pain, she allowed her anger to mire her in depression, anorexia, and self-pity. Again and again Vicki replayed the question in her mind, "Why are You punishing me, God?"

Shaking a fist in anger is a common response in our journey through grief. After all, God created anger, and He doesn't expect us to ignore it. Although Vicki's anger was justifiable, she misapplied it.

Jonah was another angry person who took it out on God. When Jonah went to Nineveh, the people turned from their evil ways, and God didn't destroy the city. Jonah hated the Ninevites and responded with displeasure and anger. In essence he pointed his finger at God, asking why. He didn't realize that four fingers were pointing back at himself. Maybe that's why God asked Jonah if he had good reason to be angry (Jonah 4:9). God wanted Jonah to examine whether he had legitimate cause for his angry feelings.

Before we express anger toward God, maybe we need to listen to His questions to us: "Do you have good reason to be angry?"

Anger can manifest itself in a variety of ways: depression, eating disorders, compulsive behavior, and so forth. It may cause us to blame and misapply our anger at God, ourselves, or others. We may need the help of a professional to guide us through the storms of our emotions and help us to cope. And we may need to seek the Maker of our emotions to heal our hurts and calm our soul.

When Jesus invited the disciples to leave the crowd and join Him on the boat, they did. I can almost hear their laughter as they ventured out on the water that day. The conditions were perfect, not a wave in sight. Then, without warning, furious waves broke over the boat, and it was nearly swamped. Would they drown? Death was near. They could feel it. They could taste it.

What was Jesus doing in the midst of this disaster? Sleeping! They woke Him and said to Him, "Teacher, don't You care if we drown?" Can you hear the terror in their voices? But if you listen closely, can you also hear the anger?

I can only imagine how they must have felt toward Jesus at this moment of crisis. Did they feel abandoned? Did they yell at Him? Did they blame Him for asking them to come on the boat in the first place? Did they have a good reason to feel angry?

As I think about the waves of emotions that can swamp us when we lose a loved one, I'm reminded of that story. In the midst of the storm, the disciples called Jesus ... and He came. He awoke, rebuked the wind, and said to the waves, "Quiet! Be still!" Then the wind died down, and all was calm.

After several years, Vicki realized that God wasn't punishing her but was the One who really understood her anger and fear. Seven years after Rew's death, Vicki knew she couldn't survive her journey through grief alone. Although she had attended church for most of her life, she had never established a personal relationship with Jesus Christ. She knew she needed Him. Vicki cried out to Jesus to come into her life, to forgive her for her sins, and to become her Lord and Savior. And He did.

He replaced Vicki's rage with hope. Although she had reason to be angry, she now knew Someone to walk with her through her personal storms of grief and to still the waves engulfing her soul.

What about you? Do you have a good reason to feel angry? Are you handling your anger in an appropriate way, or is it raging out of control? Who can help you calm your emotions?

Lord, I don't understand why You allowed the loss of my loved one. I feel as if I have good reason to vent, but I'm not sure how to express my emotions. Forgive me for hurting myself or others. I can't do this alone. You are my Maker, and I need You to guide me safely through the waves of these emotions and direct me to people who can help me. Amen.

MY PERSONAL JOURNEY

_____

_____

_____

_____

_____

_____

_____

_____

_____

_____

_____

_____

_____

_____

HIDDEN LONGINGS

All my longings lie open before you, O Lord; my sighing is not hidden from you.

PSALM 38:9

I HAVE A PAINTING in my home that I've named "Hidden Longings." A pioneer woman is standing alone in a meadow, gazing across a lake to a cabin nestled in the woods. No one else is pictured, but you can tell by the curls of smoke from the chimney that someone lives there. The woman appears to be stranded, unable to cross the lake.

Although you can't see her face, I've often imagined what she might look like and what she might be thinking. I've envisioned tears steaming down her face as she longs to be with the people who live just across the lake. Other times she has a solemn, reflective look on her face as she recalls memories with her loved ones in the cabin. Some days she looks scared and anxious because the cabin is her future and she doesn't know how to get there from where she is.

Then one day it occurred to me that she could be red-faced and angry about her loss. "Why did my loved one have to die and leave me alone? I want things back the way they were!" she shouts.

Expectations fuel our longings. When we desire something and it doesn't happen, our unfulfilled expectations lead to disappointment and pain. We long for things to be different, for our loved one to be alive, for our pain to go away. Our longings spark our emotions.

My unfulfilled expectation of watching my son grow up has been a painful disappointment. I've longed for things to be different, and my longings have sparked many hidden emotions during my journey through grief. At times I've pictured myself as the woman in the picture, crying, reflecting, fretting, and yes, venting. I've snapped at my family, slammed doors, and shouted at the top of my lungs alone in my bedroom.

Like the woman in the picture, I realize that grief is such a solitary journey. Although I wish others could understand what I feel and could walk a portion of my grief journey for me, they can't.

During those lonely times of venting I see myself as the woman calling out to God, the Master of the cabin. He opens the door and walks across the lake to meet me where I am. Then He wraps His arms around me and holds me. He allows me to cast my cares on Him and release my anger. He listens. He is Jehovah Rapha to me, which means "the Lord who heals." He understands my hidden longings and my anger. He heals my broken heart and binds up my wounds.

Maybe you see yourself like the woman in the picture, longing for your loved one and wishing he or she were still alive. Reflecting about your past. Anxious about the future. Or red-faced and angry. It's okay to feel any of those emotions. But you don't have to be alone. Call out to God to join you. He understands your hidden longings and your pain and will allow you to cast your cares and anger on Him. He will meet you where you are today. Call on Him now.

God, inside I'm red-faced and angry about my loss and the changes it has forced upon me. I'm standing alone, gazing at the cabin that I can't reach. I'm anxious about the future and don't know how to get there. Please come to me now. I don't want to be alone in my pain. Help me release my hidden longings to You today. You are Jehovah Rapha, the Lord who heals. Please heal my broken heart and bind up my wounds today so I can release my anger and journey on. Amen.

My Personal Journey

Devotion 10

JETTY OF CALM

■ ■ ■

When anxiety was great within me, your consolation brought joy to my soul.

THE OCEAN CAPTIVATES ME. It's massive and mysterious yet soothing and predictable. Its waves can rage fiercely yet lap calmly against the shore. It can destroy cities and lives yet provide entertainment and food. The ocean is ever changing.

That's why we hired an experienced seaman to take us on a deep-sea fishing adventure. He understood the ocean and knew how to maneuver his boat and how to keep us safe. When we boarded the boat and began to sail through the harbor, I was amazed how calm and smooth the water was. Then I noticed a structure extending out into the sea that the waves were crashing against and asked the seaman about it. "It's a jetty," he said. "It protects the harbor from the ocean."

A few moments later, I knew what he meant as we left the harbor and steered into the ocean. Our boat rocked and swayed; waves crashed and my stomach churned. I lost my balance and fell down. I got sick. With my head tucked between my knees, I kept thinking about the smooth, calm water in the harbor, behind the jetty's protection.

Your grief journey is a bit like the ocean. Some days grief feels massive and mysterious, yet on other days it seems calm and under control.

At times you may even take precautions and seek out experts who understand grief. They know how to maneuver you safely through the ocean swell of emotions. For even though your journey has its smooth spots, eventually, you realize the waves of your emotions are getting choppier. You begin to lash out at others. Your stomach churns. You feel sick. Your anger rages on. You want to be calm again and shielded from the fury. You need a personal jetty.

When you consider the acts of kindness, encouraging cards, timely phone calls, songs that soothe, and prayers that others offer on your behalf, could it be that God has designed them as jetties to calm your grieving soul? He understands the depth of your pain, and He might use these simple acts to protect you from your raging emotions. He cares about you and will provide unexpected peace and shelter when you need it. Call on Him. Thank Him for being your shield and for the people He has provided to calm your soul. Ask Him to help you find shelter in the jetties He provides today.

God, I'm sailing through the ocean of grief. Some days the grief feels massive and mysterious. Some days I can cope and am calm. Other days my emotions are choppy and are raging out of control. Help me, Lord. Soothe my soul. Allow me to find shelter in the jetties that You provide for me today. Thank You for being my shield and for providing others to encourage me.

MY PERSONAL JOURNEY

_____

_____

_____

_____

MY PERSONAL JOURNEY

YOUR JOURNEY THROUGH QUESTIONING

Questioning: *to cross-examine, doubt, dispute, examine, analyze, inquire.*

■ ■ ■

The "why" of so many things
Is sometimes known only to the heart of God.
But He has promised us . . .
that at all times,
in all places,
and in all circumstances,
nothing can separate us from His love.

AUTHOR UNKNOWN

For I am convinced that neither death nor life, neither angels nor demons, neither the present nor the future, nor any powers, neither height nor depth, nor anything else in all creation, will be able to separate us from the love of God that is in Christ Jesus our Lord.

ROMANS 8:38–39

Devotion 11

WANDERING THROUGH THE
WILDERNESS OF "WHY"

■ ■ ■

Then the LORD answered Job out of the storm. He said: "Who is this that darkens my counsel with words without knowledge? Brace yourself like a man; I will question you, and you shall answer me."

JOB 38:1–3

"MOMMY, WHY DO ALL our babies have to die?" The question left me speechless. How should I respond to my brokenhearted son, who had prayed so fervently that God would give us a baby? Should I tell him that I didn't understand either?

The "whys" began to whirl around in my mind: Why, after a miscarriage, years of infertility, and adopting our son, had I become pregnant again only to discover that our baby had a fatal defect and would die shortly after birth? Why did I become pregnant a third time just months after losing our infant son only to miscarry this third baby? And why must I face my son tonight, on Christmas Eve, and tell him I am losing a fourth baby? So many whys and so few answers.

Silence pervaded the room as my son waited for my response. I grasped for the right words, but none came. At first I felt uncomfortable, not knowing the answer to his question. Then I realized that was the answer.

"Jake, I don't know. All I know is God is there, God is good, and that's enough."

I felt relieved to finally admit, "God, I don't get it!"

Too often the wicked seem to strike it rich while godly servants struggle. The lazy employee lies yet is promoted, while the hardworking, deserving one is ignored. A dead baby is carelessly dumped at the prom while a godly couple who desperately desire children hold their dying infant. A man abuses his body with drugs while a young, health-conscious father dies of cancer and leaves behind a wife and children.

What we think about God will influence how we respond to trials in this lifetime. If we feel that Job's loss of his family, possessions, and health was something Satan slipped by while God was busy elsewhere or that Job's loss was unavoidable . . . think again! If we see God as the God of the Bible, sovereign, supreme, sensitive, not allowing death and trials except by divine permission, then we can see purpose, even if we don't know what that purpose is.

Most of us who are in the journey of grieving someone we love may not have answers to why. During times of questioning I reflect on Job's life and remember that no suffering can touch the believer without having first received God's permission. I must filter my loss through the lens of deity and not my human sight.

Are you wandering through the wilderness of Why? God understands. He is good. He is there. Sometimes that's the only answer there is.

God, even though I don't understand why this happened and maybe never will, I still know You are trustworthy. You are good. You are in control. I may not know what the future holds, but I do know who holds the future. As I continue to wander through the wilderness of Why, help me to trust You and not to lean on my own understanding. Amen.

MY PERSONAL JOURNEY

_____

_____

_____

My Personal Journey

_____
_____
_____
_____
_____
_____
_____
_____
_____
_____
_____
_____
_____
_____
_____
_____
_____
_____
_____
_____
_____
_____

Devotion 12

THE MYSTERY OF DEATH'S TIMING

■ ■ ■

There is a time for everything, and a season for every activity under heaven: a time to be born and a time to die, a time to plant and a time to uproot, a time to kill and a time to heal, a time to tear down and a time to build, a time to weep and a time to laugh, a time to mourn and a time to dance, a time to scatter stones and a time to gather them, a time to embrace and a time to refrain, a time to search and a time to give up, a time to keep and a time to throw away, a time to tear and a time to mend, a time to be silent and a time to speak, a time to love and a time to hate, a time for war and a time for peace.

ECCLESIASTES 3:1–8

DEATH'S TIMING IS A mystery. It intrudes into our lives and snatches away our loved one. Like a detective, we feel a desperate need to solve our case, to understand why. We sift through clues, search for evidence, and examine all of death's possible motives for seizing our loved one. Frustration fuels our investigation. We seek answers to our questions but find none.

"Why now?" we ask. Death came much too soon. It left dreams undone, life unlived, words unspoken.

We may never solve the why of "the when." Yet, like Solomon, we may need to consider there is a time and season for everything, and we are to savor every moment.

That's what Alice discovered one morning in her backyard as she sought answers and peace. The past few weeks' events had touched her soul deeply. As she strolled through the grass, she recalled how her grandson had died just moments after his birth. How odd that birth and death could come so close together. Yet his brief life had changed hers forever. She mourned the loss of never being a granny who read to him, baked him cookies, taught him to fish, drank hot chocolate with him under a moonlit sky, or watched her daughter be a mother to him.

As Alice continued to walk, she longed for a time to heal. Then she saw a green, celery-like stem with fragile, transparent blossoms coming out of the ground. The flower hadn't been there yesterday. She remembered the previous fall planting a bulb her friend had given to her, calling it "a surprise lily."

A few days later, Alice walked again in the backyard and found the blossoms had died. Disappointed, she told her friend about the short-lived bloom only to discover that the normal life span for that type of lily was a few days.

Why would God create something so beautiful and allow it to die so quickly? Alice wondered. Her thoughts drifted to her grandchild. She reflected on the joy she had felt over his coming and her disappointment over his short life. She walked over to her patio, opened her Bible, and read, "Teach us to number our days and recognize how few they are; help us to spend them as we should" (Psalm 90:12, TLB).

God's truth penetrated her soul. Although many of her questions still remained unanswered, she sensed a deeper appreciation for life — whether it be brief or long.

Like Alice, the timing of our loved one's death may remain a mystery, but we can treasure every moment we are given as a gift. Let's make the most of our time today and our time with our loved ones. We never know when we or they may be gone.

Lord, Your timing is a mystery to me. I admit I don't understand why You chose to take my loved one away when You did. I wanted to experience so many things with him (her) and say so many things. I've searched for answers to my questions, but I realize there are none. Your Word says there is a time and a season for everything. I'm ready for a time of joy, peace, and healing. Help me to embrace the time You've given me and to make the most of every moment today. Amen.

My Personal Journey

STRANDED ON
"IF ONLY" ISLAND

■ ■ ■

"Lord," Martha said to Jesus, "if you had been here, my brother would not have died."

JOHN 11:21

SHE NEVER GAVE UP hope. Surely her friend would come with His healing touch. But she watched helplessly as her brother's condition worsened. She waited and prayed, waited and prayed.

After his death and the funeral was over, she felt numb, body and soul, as though she, rather than her brother, had just been laid to rest in the grave. She felt isolated and abandoned, as if she were consigned to an island in the sea, with no one to rescue her.

Then, when Martha heard that Jesus had finally come, she went out to meet Him. She recalled the laughter and conversation they had shared along this path. But this homecoming was different. Her brother Lazarus was dead. Martha's red, puffy eyes were filled with hurt and disappointment. She had so many questions to ask.

Stopping in front of Jesus, her eyes locked with His. "Lord, if You had been here, my brother would not have died. But I know that even now God will give You whatever You ask."

Jesus must have sensed Martha's hope amidst her hurt and assured her that her brother would rise again. Martha nodded in agreement; she was accustomed to extraordinary things happening when He was around. But did she anticipate what Jesus would do that day? She watched Him weep. She knew He cared deeply and felt the pain of loss. She wondered if His anguish was what drove Him to open the tomb and to cry out for Lazarus. Yet, even as she followed Him to Lazarus's grave, Martha was consumed by the thought, "If only. . . ."

Like Martha, maybe you've said, "Lord, if only You had been here, my loved one wouldn't have died." Someone you loved was facing death, and you cried out to Jesus for help. You prayed. You waited. You claimed His promises. But still, he died. Perhaps you've had regrets about what unfolded. You've thought, *If only I had prayed harder . . . If only I had encouraged him to go to the doctor sooner . . . If only the accident had never occurred . . . If only the Lord had come and saved him.*

If only . . . if only . . . if only.

"If only" thinking can destroy us emotionally and spiritually. Too often we equate God's healing with His presence and death with His absence. When a loved one dies, we feel abandoned or even punished. Such conclusions can make us feel hopeless and angry, resentful and bitter. We blame instead of believe. And then we end up on If Only Island.

If you feel stranded on your own If Only Island, imagine for a moment that you notice a ship in the distance. It sails closer, and then Jesus steps ashore to greet you. You stomp over to confront Him with your questions, but He answers only with His tears. Only with His embrace. He understands what it feels like to cry out and not to be rescued. He knows how it feels to be deserted and abandoned. In His own body, He has experienced the pain of death.

As He reaches out His hands to you, you notice the nail marks. You hear Him say, "If only you would come to Me, I would give you rest. If only you would believe that I am always with you. If only you would cast all your cares on Me because I care for you. If only you would let go of your 'if onlys' and trust Me with all your heart."

Yes, if only.

Lord, death is so difficult and so confusing. There's so much I don't understand. But You do. I'm tired of blaming You for not coming to the res-

cue. I don't want to entertain "if only" thinking anymore. Please replace my blaming with believing. Help me to surrender my questions and cares. Bring me back from my lonely island of questioning and anger and restore my hope. Amen.

❧

My Personal Journey

_____

_____

_____

_____

_____

_____

_____

_____

_____

_____

_____

_____

_____

_____

_____

_____

Devotion 14

WHY NOT ME?

■ ■ ■

"For my thoughts are not your thoughts, neither are your ways my ways,"
declares the LORD. "As the heavens are higher than the earth, so are my ways
higher than your ways and my thoughts than your thoughts."

ISAIAH 55:8—9

ONE DAY AS I watched the news, I heard about Kevin and Penny. They
had planned to be together in marriage. Instead, they were united in
death, buried side by side after a tornado ravaged their town. Just a few
blocks away from the cemetery, another family and group of friends gathered for a funeral service for Niles, a young child who was sucked from
his father's arms by the same violent twister. Mourners stared at the
miniature white casket trimmed with blue lace and a pair of his "Sesame
Street" socks with the words, "Why? Why? Why?" printed on them.

Death at any hour is sad and difficult to deal with, but when it comes
without warning, it brings jarring surprise with it. No one expects to
receive a phone call telling her that her teenager was just killed, or that
the plane crash had no survivors, or that a bomb exploded in the building where her loved one worked. Newspapers and newscasts abound
with stories like these.

I've come to realize that behind every headline, news story, or obit-
uary are people who have lost a loved one — a parent, child, neighbor,
coworker, or friend. All too often in the past, I responded inappropri-
ately to grieving people. But experiencing loss firsthand has sharpened
my awareness.

Now I wish reporters would be more sensitive to the bereaved. I've watched in disbelief as the camera zooms in on a victim's family and a microphone is shoved in their faces while the reporter probes, "Do you understand why this happened?" They usually respond with silence or sobs. However, when one mother was interviewed after her son had been killed, her reply was, "Why not me?" The reporter was startled. The woman acknowledged that, although she didn't understand the whys of her son's death, she was more puzzled about why God had allowed her to live.

Why not me in the obituaries today? Why not me in the fatal accident? Why not me in the tragic headlines? The more I reflect on it, the more humbled I am at God's sovereignty and plans for each of our lives.

God's ways are not our ways.

Maybe that's what Mary thought as she watched her Son take His last breath. What a tragic death it was. He didn't deserve to die. He was loving, kind, blameless.

I wonder how His story would have appeared on the evening news. The camera zooms in on a Man nailed to a cross. Perspiration and blood trickle down His body. He cries out, gasps, and His body falls limp. The reporter shoves the microphone into Mary's tearstained face and asks her to describe how she feels. I can only imagine her anguish as Joseph of Arimathea and Nicodemus remove her Son's body from the cross. She lovingly cradles His body in her arms and runs her fingers through His blood-soaked hair. She takes a deep breath, gulps, and looks straight into the camera as she responds, "Why not me?"

What about you? Are you in the midst of questioning and trying to understand the whys of your loss? Striving for answers is a normal part of grief. But have you ever considered asking a different question: "Why not me?"

Lord, I don't understand why things have happened this way. I may never comprehend the reason tragedies occur in this life. Obviously, Your ways are not my ways. You demonstrated that when You died on the cross.

You were innocent. I was guilty. Why not me on the cross? Thank You for loving me so much that You took my place. You are the Way, the Truth, the Life. You are the answer to my questions. Amen.

MY PERSONAL JOURNEY

_____

_____

_____

_____

_____

_____

_____

_____

_____

_____

_____

_____

_____

_____

_____

FROM TRAGEDY
TO TRIUMPH

■ ■ ■

Now I want you to know, brothers, that what has happened to me has really served to advance the gospel.

PHILIPPIANS 1:12

ONE CHRISTMAS EVE KAREN walked up the old farmhouse's creaky steps. Deciding to move to the country and to enjoy a simpler lifestyle was a gift both she and her husband were glad they had decided to give their family. In just a few short months, surrounded by pigs and chickens, they had made a lifetime of memories.

Karen tiptoed down the hall to the bedroom where her daughters were sleeping. She bent down and gently kissed their foreheads. *How lucky I am to be their mom*, she thought.

She smiled as she recalled how cute they had looked in the Christmas play, with their enthusiastically loud voices belting out "Away in a Manger." She could hardly wait to see their beaming faces on Christmas morning as they opened their gifts beneath the tree.

Moments later Karen cuddled next to her husband and drifted off to sleep. Her dreams turned to nightmares when she and Willie awoke to a crackling noise. They descended the stairs. Flames were everywhere. *I have to get the girls*, Karen thought. She raced up the steps toward their room, but she couldn't penetrate the dense, black fog pouring out of the doorway. "Rachel, Ruthie, get up!" she screamed. But there was no response.

Willie bolted through the darkness. Karen knew he would come running out with the girls. But he didn't. The intense heat was burning Karen's skin and hair as she gasped for air. There was no escape. *Help me, God! Should I stay or should I go?* Then she remembered the ladder in her bedroom for emergencies. She crashed through the window and climbed down to safety.

By this time, the fire was raging out of control. Karen was numb with disbelief, and the emptiness she felt was beyond description. Her entire family was gone. She questioned why this tragedy had happened and how she would survive beyond it.

If we look at circumstances from a human point of view, we have good reason to question and despair. It's normal to question the loss of a loved one. It's natural to wonder how we will survive without him or her. We don't understand the big picture and why God allowed something so terrible to happen.

Jesus Himself asked the question, "My God, my God, why have you forsaken me?" when He was dying on a Roman cross. When He did, He gave us permission to cry out to God in our grief.

From a human point of view, Jesus' death was a tragedy. Yet, what looked like a devastating setback was in spiritual reality a turning point in history. In the same way, God can transform our questions, suffering, and circumstance into a gift to others who are questioning.

Tragedies can result in modern-day triumphs. That's what happened when a beautiful, vibrant, athletic young woman had an accident that permanently paralyzed her from the neck down. "Terrible," we say. And we're right. "Her life is ruined," we decide. And we're wrong! Through that accident Joni Eareckson Tada became a great gift to the church and found a new and fulfilling life for herself. Tragedy became triumph.

A young woman who was raped and became pregnant later took the post of director of a crisis pregnancy center. Tragedy again turned to triumph.

After a season of grieving the loss of her family, Karen met a compassionate man, remarried, and had twins. Although her new family would never replace the family she had lost and her questions remained unanswered, she didn't turn away from her pain but instead turned to God. She began to share her story through musical concerts to give hope to the hurting. She allowed God to transform her tragedy into triumph.

When tragedies strike (and they will), the apostle Paul urges us to look past the circumstance. What seems like defeat may turn into victory, what looks like suffering may become joy, and what appears to be a tragedy may lead to spiritual triumph.

Lord, thank You for Your patience with me and for giving me permission to ask why, just as Jesus did. Fill my mind with Your perspective and make my loss and suffering count for something good that will help others who are questioning. Amen.

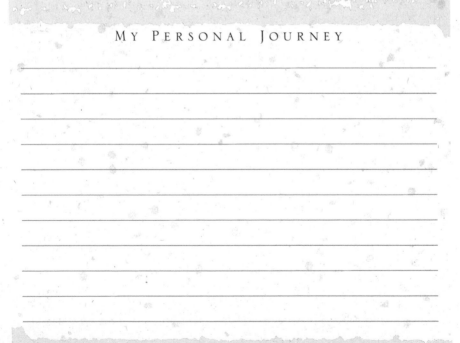

MY PERSONAL JOURNEY

My Personal Journey

YOUR JOURNEY THROUGH BARGAINING

Bargaining: *to negotiate, haggle; to come to terms; to agree, barter.*

■ ■ ■

The altar is not a bargain counter where you haggle with God. With Him it is all or nothing.

LANCE ZAVITZ

In bitterness of soul Hannah wept much and prayed to the LORD. And she made a vow, saying, "O LORD Almighty, if you will only look upon your servant's misery and remember me, and not forget your servant but give her a son, then I will give him to the LORD for all the days of his life, and no razor will ever be used on his head."

1 SAMUEL 1:10–11

Be careful what you promise in prayer because God
      may take you up on it.
Are you willing to follow through on any promise you
      make if God grants your request?

AUTHOR UNKNOWN

JOURNEY TO THE MARKETPLACE
OF BARGAINING

■ ■ ■

I can do everything through him who gives me strength.

PHILIPPIANS 4:13

I GREW UP IN a family of small business owners. My grandfather owned the town's general store, my Uncle June was the postmaster, my dad owned the gas station, my mom owned the beauty parlor, and my Uncle Bob owned the funeral home. I believed that our family could do everything. All we needed was a preacher in the family, and our slogan could be, "We can do it all . . . from marry to bury." From this rural beginning, I learned the necessity of good customer service and the importance of bargaining, developing techniques and incentives to entice people to buy.

Sales and marketing were a natural career path for me, and I thrived during the fifteen years I spent in media advertising sales. Problem solving and negotiating were my specialties.

When my sales manager proposed a sales contest with a trip to San Francisco as a prize, I was determined to win. I strategically planned how to make my presentation and to overcome any possible objections a client might have. I strolled into my first client's office the next day and shared the opportunity. He wasn't convinced. I rebutted his objections. I was about to give up when I remembered an additional incentive I thought I could talk my boss into giving. It worked! He bought it.

Now the only hurdle was to convince my sales manager to accept my conditions. Unfortunately, she rejected my proposal. I was disappointed at the time, but looking back I'm glad she did because my client ended up going out of business. His failure would have cost me the trip (which I ended up winning anyway) and my commission.

Sometimes in our journey through grief we think we know it all and persist in negotiating with God about our loss. Like a bargaining salesperson, we employ techniques and propose incentives to God to sweeten the deal — or at least to lessen the pain. We rebut His objections and go for the close, but often He rejects our proposal. We may feel disappointed, even angry. Yet He sees beyond our short-term request. He understands the overall plan and has a reason for saying no to us. Over time we may start to understand, but even if we don't, God does. When we exchange our "I can do it all" thinking for "I can do all things through Christ who strengthens me" thinking, we are well on our way to moving on in our journey through grief.

God, sometimes I think, "I can do it all" without Your help in my journey through grief. I propose solutions, negotiate, and even offer You incentives to accept my terms, but often You reject them. Please forgive me for being disappointed and angry with You. Help me to accept Your answers even though I may not understand them. You are the God who sees the future. Be my strength. Help me to trust You today with my loss and to quit bargaining with You.

MY PERSONAL JOURNEY

My Personal Journey

FATHER KNOWS BEST

Trust in the LORD with all your heart and lean not on your own understanding; in all your ways acknowledge him, and he will make your paths straight.

PROVERBS 3:5—6

WHEN KING HEZEKIAH DISCOVERED he was about to die, his grief drove him through the gates of bargaining. He prayed to God and reminded Him of his faithfulness and good deeds. He wept bitterly as he faced death. Hezekiah obviously didn't agree with God's decision and bargained for a different one. In this situation, God did grant Hezekiah's request and extended his life. However, there's more to the story than meets the eye.

God added fifteen years to Hezekiah's life, but during that time Manasseh, his son, was born. Manasseh became the most wicked king in Israel's history. Yes, God granted Hezekiah's request, but it might have been better if He hadn't!

Grief may drive us to bargain with God. Sharing honest feelings with God is healthy, and He wants us to cast our hurts and cares on Him. But when we're tempted to tell Him how to do His job, we might want to stop and remember Hezekiah. Rather than plead for our way, perhaps we should simply say, "God, only if it's for the best." We don't see the future, but God does. He is all-knowing and sovereign. Even though we may not understand, He is our Father, and He knows best.

God, sometimes I wish I could change the outcome of my circumstances. I want to be in control. Please forgive me for telling You how to do Your job. Even though I don't understand, I know You must have a reason. Help me trust You. I release my fear, uncertainty, and conditions to You today. Grant my desire only if it's for the best. Amen.

My Personal Journey

My Personal Journey

Devotion 18

GOD DELIVERED MORE THAN I BARGAINED FOR

∎ ∎ ∎

Now to him who is able to do immeasurably more than all we ask or imagine, according to his power that is at work within us, to him be glory in the church and in Christ Jesus to all generations, for ever and ever! Amen.

EPHESIANS 3:20–21

"KATH, I'VE BEEN IN a car accident. I'm in the emergency room in Baltimore."

My heart froze. "Rich, what happened?"

"I was knocked unconscious and brought here by helicopter. Kath, they had to cut off my new suit...." My husband's voice cracked as he fought back tears.

I tightly clutched the receiver. I should be there with him right now, not two thousand miles away in Phoenix. I felt helpless, yet I knew that I needed to be strong. I soothed him with words. I prayed with him over the phone that God would be his peace, protector, and comforter, and would take care of every detail of this situation ... including getting me there.

"Good-bye, Kath," were Rich's final words in our conversation. I replayed them in my mind and wondered if these would be his last. *God, You've already taken my son. Please don't take my husband too*, I pleaded. I relived my fear and anguish when I had begged God to spare my son. I knew God was capable of sparing him, but God had chosen not to in spite of my bargaining. Now would I have to endure another loss just six months later?

Only God knew.

At that moment all I knew was that I had to trust God, even though I wanted to tell Him how to do His job. My husband was in His hands.

Then I watched as God worked out every detail. Relief enveloped me when I walked into the intensive care unit and heard Rich say, "Hello." His private nurse assured me that he would recover from his broken ribs, bruises, and concussion.

Two days later, Rich was released from the hospital, and his company's special treatment overwhelmed us. A coworker transported us to the Marriott Hotel. Wheelchair service whisked us to our hotel suite, and we enjoyed room service between naps. When the chef came to our room to personally serve our food and to inquire about Rich, we wondered what God would do next.

Well, the first-class seats and a nonstop flight home to Phoenix minimized Rich's pain. Then I picked up our son and discovered my friend had laundered his clothes and even purchased his next day's school supplies. God cared about every detail!

Just when I thought God was finished, He surprised us again. All expenses incurred for this trip, including the new suit the hospital attendants had cut off Rich, would be covered by his company. God even provided a souvenir from this experience — a two-inch remnant of blue fabric — as far as we know, the only remains of Rich's suit.

We've kept that remnant to encourage us during times of uncertainty in our grief journey, to remind us that God is faithful. He may not always answer our requests in the way we desire, but when we trust Him with the details, He will give us more than we bargained for.

Pleading and bargaining with God are such a normal part of the grief journey. Yet your bargain may not be one God can accept. You may even be tempted to think God hasn't heard you pleading. But remember, for a moment, the cross, and you'll realize that Jesus didn't bargain with God. Instead He surrendered Himself in unconditional love. And you reaped the benefits. God gave you much more than you bargained for.

God, sometimes You answer my prayers differently than I asked You to. My conditions aren't always part of Your plans. I don't understand Your ways, and I don't want to endure pain and loss. Help me to trust You with the details of my life. Replace my conditions with Your unconditional love. Thank You for sacrificing Your life for me and for giving me more than I bargained for — eternal hope. Show me how to trust You today. Amen.

MY PERSONAL JOURNEY

LET'S MAKE A DEAL

■ ■ ■

*"For I know the plans I have for you," declares the LORD, "plans to prosper
you and not to harm you, plans to give you hope and a future."*

JEREMIAH 29:11

"DO YOU WANT TO trade what you have for what's behind door number
one, door number two, or door number three?" I remember hearing
Monty Hall's words offering contestants an opportunity to bargain with
him on the television game show, *Let's Make a Deal*. Some contestants
were content with their prizes and wouldn't trade them while others
were quick to respond and take the risk. Their bargaining sometimes
resulted in an undesired prize like a pet goat or a bathtub on wheels.
Had they known what they were bargaining for, they would have made
a different decision.

Often in our grief journey we may want to exchange our loss for
something else. We approach God and ask Him to make a deal with us.

When Jacob heard that Joseph was dead, he mourned for many
days. This wasn't an outcome he desired; his favorite son was dead. I
wonder if he bargained with God and presented other options.
Exchange my life for his . . . take one of my other sons instead . . . take
all of my possessions, but bring him back.

Jacob had experience bargaining with people. He had traded food
for his brother's birthright. He had made a deal with Laban to work for
him seven years so Jacob could marry Rachel, only to be tricked and

receive her older sister, Leah, instead. Disheartened yet persistent, Jacob agreed to work seven more years in exchange for Rachel.

Although Jacob had experience in bargaining with people, making a deal with God was different. When Jacob learned of his son's death, God seemed unresponsive. But, in fact, He was busily preparing a surprise behind a door that wouldn't be opened for many years.

Several years later, when a famine struck Israel, Jacob sent his sons to Egypt for food. Little did he know that his needs would be supplied by his "dead" son Joseph, who, rather than dying all those years ago had been sold into slavery by his brothers. By then Joseph had been promoted to a position of authority in Egypt. When the famine struck his family, Joseph was used by God to save them.

I wonder how this story would have ended had Jacob bargained successfully with God. Unlike people who don't always have our best interests in mind or see the big picture, God always does. He sees beyond the door of our grief to the bigger plan and purpose. He cares about our future and wants the best for us and others even though we may not comprehend at the time what He is doing.

Unlike game shows, making deals with God can be risky. You may think you want to exchange the pain of your loss for something else, but if you really knew the future and what the outcome would be, you might reconsider. Only God knows the purpose of your loss. Only He sees the future behind door number one, two, and three. In spite of your questions and pain, are you willing to exchange your limited knowledge and let's-make-a-deal attitude for God's sovereignty? Maybe it's time to. He's waiting for you to accept His offer. Why not acknowledge His sovereignty today?

God, I've been trying to make a deal with You about my loss. It feels like a booby prize, and I want to exchange it for something else. I can't see the purpose behind my door of loss. Your Word says that You know the plans and the purposes for my life and that You desire the best for me. I want to believe that, but sometimes it's hard. Forgive me for trying to control the outcome by bargaining with You. I acknowledge that You are sovereign and that You see the big picture of my life and loss. Help me to trust You today with my uncertainty and exchange my let's-make-a-deal attitude for Your peace. Amen.

MY PERSONAL JOURNEY

_____

_____

_____

_____

_____

_____

_____

_____

_____

_____

_____

_____

_____

_____

BARGAINING WITH UNCERTAINTY
ABOUT YOUR LOVED ONE'S
ETERNAL FUTURE

■ ■ ■

*For it is by grace you have been saved, through faith — and this not from
yourselves, it is the gift of God — not by works, so that no one can boast.*

EPHESIANS 2:8

*For God so loved the world that he gave his one and only Son, that whoever
believes in him shall not perish but have eternal life.*

JOHN 3:16

WE ALL WANT TO believe our loved ones are in heaven. It comforts us
and brings closure to our grief knowing that someday we will see them
again. But all too often I've observed well-meaning pastors, family, and
friends speak about a person's heavenly future without knowing for certain whether it's true.

How do we know if our loved one is in heaven? Can we make that
judgment? And how do we cope with the uncertainty of not knowing?

Picturing our loved ones anywhere besides heaven is distressing.
Dealing with their deaths is painful enough, but living with the uncertainty of their eternal future can overwhelm us. To cope, we may find
ourselves bargaining with others and with God about our loved one's
eternal future. "But she was a good person"; "He went to church and
was always helping others"; "Even though she didn't talk about God, I'm
sure she must have loved Him"; "If God is a loving God, then He
wouldn't turn His back on my loved one." We desperately grasp for certainty to end our turmoil. Like a present, we want to wrap up our loved

87

one's life in bright paper, tape it together with good works and justifications, and top it off with a bow of certainty — eternal life with God.

I wonder if that's what James and John's mother was thinking when she approached Jesus and bargained with Him about her sons' eternal positions. She must have wanted to do everything within her power to put a bow on their future, even if it meant pleading and negotiating. How discouraged she must have felt when Jesus responded, "You don't know what you are asking. . . . Can you drink the cup I am going to drink? . . . You will indeed drink from my cup, but to sit at my right or left is not for me to grant. These places belong to those for whom they have been prepared by my Father" (Matthew 20:22–23).

We cannot secure another person's place in heaven or his or her eternal future regardless how hard we plead, justify, or bargain with God. Some things, like our loved one's future, are out of our control. Nothing we can do can change it.

Yet, amidst this uncertainty we can cling to an eternal God who is merciful beyond our understanding. And His Word promises that everyone who lives will be given an opportunity to reject or receive His free gift of eternal life. One thing is certain: Before your loved one died, he or she did hear the truth and had an opportunity to respond. Could it have happened on her deathbed, while she was in a coma, or in a supernatural way? Absolutely. With God all things are possible. He wants no one to perish but everyone to live eternally with Him.

Will you see your loved one in heaven? Only God knows. But more importantly, will you spend eternity with God? That free gift is waiting for you to reject or receive. Put the bow of certainty on your eternal future today.

Lord, I can't imagine never seeing my loved one again. I hope he (she) is in heaven with You. I commit my uncertainty about his (her) future to You today. Thank You that You provide a way for everyone who lives to hear the truth and to reject or receive Your gift of eternal life. Thank You that my loved one had that opportunity. I want to know with certainty that I will spend eternity with You. I believe You are the only way to have eternal life and that You died on the cross for my sins. You conquered death and rose again and are preparing a place for me and others who receive You. Come into my life. Amen.

❧

MY PERSONAL JOURNEY

_____

_____

_____

_____

_____

_____

_____

_____

_____

_____

_____

_____

_____

_____

_____

_____

_____

MY PERSONAL JOURNEY

YOUR JOURNEY THROUGH CRYING

Crying: *an utterance of distress, rage, or pain; sobbing, weeping, releasing tears.*

There is a time and season for tears.
When your heart is full of anguish,
they begin to flow as naturally as raindrops from heaven.
There is a hidden beauty in tears, a welcome cleansing
     about them.
They should be shed boldly in public or in solitude.
They symbolize how much you have loved and lost.
Tears commemorate and celebrate your loved ones.
There is a holiness about your tears.
Each one is a prayer that only God can understand.
He created them and shed them Himself.
They are His reminder to you that your soul can have
     no rainbows,
if your eyes can have no tears.

KATHE WUNNENBERG

FACING THE FLASH
FLOODS OF TEARS

Record my lament; list my tears on your scroll — are they not in your record?

PSALM 56:8

WHEN TOO MUCH PRESSURE is put on the heart, tears are its safety valve. No matter how hard we try to control ourselves, sometimes there's just no stopping them. Though we may try to sandbag our emotions, sooner or later the wall breaks, and the tears come flooding through.

They may erupt when we hear a favorite song, smell a familiar cologne, or see a family picture and remember how much we miss our loved one. Tears are unpredictable. They may surface in the middle of the night, in the middle of the grocery store, or in the middle of a conversation. Sometimes they come for no apparent reason at all.

One "flash flood" occurred for me at an out-of-state conference. Fifteen of us had gathered in the living room of a turn-of-the-century mansion for our closing session. Though strangers when we had arrived just days earlier, I realized by the constant buzz of conversation that friendships had already been kindled. When the leader signaled it was time to begin, I noticed she had placed a large, antique chair in the middle of the room. One by one she asked each of us to take our turn sitting in the chair while the rest of us showered that person with encouraging words and prayer.

When my turn came, I sat down and looked at the caring eyes that surrounded me. Something about this felt familiar. Immediately I began to weep.

Why was I reacting this way? Then it hit me. The last time I had sat in a circle like this had been a month before my baby's death. My friends had gathered to give me an "encouragement shower" to help me face my baby's birth and impending death. My flashback triggered a flash flood.

That's the mystery of grief; it's personal and unique. No two people grieve exactly the same way. But most (if not all) will say that the journey through the valley of tears is normal and necessary. So grab a Kleenex (or a box or two) and allow your tears to relieve the pressure from your hurting heart.

Lord, I'm crying again. Will my tears ever stop? Your ledger for my tears must be overflowing. Because You created tears and You wept when Your friend Lazarus died, I know it's okay to cry. You know my heart is breaking, and You understand my pain. Please comfort me today and help me to trust You through the flash floods of tears. Amen.

MY PERSONAL JOURNEY

_____

_____

_____

_____

_____

_____

_____

My Personal Journey

HAPPY-SAD TEARS

■ ■ ■

I have set my rainbow in the clouds, and it will be the sign of the covenant between me and the earth. Whenever I bring clouds over the earth and the rainbow appears in the clouds, I will remember my covenant between me and you and all living creatures of every kind. Never again will the waters become a flood to destroy all life. Whenever the rainbow appears in the clouds, I will see it and remember the everlasting covenant between God and all living creatures of every kind on the earth.

GENESIS 9:13—16

THE DAY OF THE anniversary of my son's death is a time I look forward to yet dread. To other people, that day on their calendars seems ordinary, but to me, each year, it's a milestone to celebrate — I have survived another year without my son.

One year, in anticipation of the day, I prepared myself for a flurry of emotions and made sure I had plenty of tissues. I carefully planned a memorable day that included a trip to the cemetery, a service project or recreational activity in honor of my son, and time alone to reflect.

I gave myself permission to cry whenever I felt like it, to think about my son, or to talk about him with others. How old would he be now? What would he be doing? What would he look like? What would his favorite book or movie be? What would his laugh sound like? How would his hug feel? What would he think about this year's family vacation? How would he and his big brother get along?

I continued to ponder. What had he learned in heaven? What was it like to be in God's presence and to have no pain, darkness, or tears? Who did he spend time with there? What was his heavenly job?

I felt a tear trickle down my cheek. I swiped the tissue across my face just as my son, Jake, walked into the room. He stood in front of me and gave me a long, questioning stare. "Mom, why are crying and smiling at the same time?"

Without thinking I blurted out, "These are happy-sad tears."

"Happy-sad tears? What do you mean, Mom?"

"Well, I'm happy because your brother is in heaven, but I'm sad because I miss him today."

Jake nodded, handed me a tissue, and gave me a reassuring hug. Amazingly, this seven-year-old boy understood and gave me permission to cry.

Later that week Jake ran into the house and screamed, "Mom, come quick!"

Fearing the worst, I bolted outside, only to discover him standing in the middle of the yard smiling as it rained. Just as I was about to ground him for scaring me, he pointed to the sky. The sun was shining through the clouds, and a rainbow was beginning to appear.

"Mom, I've never seen it rain and shine at the same time. It reminds me of happy-sad tears."

I nodded, smiled, and walked over to stand in the rain with him. I felt affirmed that tears and smiles can happen at the same time in our grief journey. Happy-sad tears are a lot like a rainbow — it takes both rain and sunshine to make a rainbow.

Maybe it's time for you to embrace your tears and smile as you journey on.

Lord, today is another milestone for me without my loved one — I've made it through another day, another week, another month. Help me to remember and celebrate his (her) life. Some of my memories make me smile and cry at the same time. I know that tears are okay and they are a necessary part of my journey through grief. Thanks for creating rainbows and happy-sad tears. Help me to see Your sunshine in the midst of my tears and to have eyes to see the rainbow through my grief. Amen.

MY PERSONAL JOURNEY

Devotion 23

"REMEMBERING" TEARS

■ ■ ■

The LORD does not look at the things man looks at. Man looks at the outward appearance, but the LORD looks at the heart.

1 SAMUEL 16:7B

HAVE YOU EVER CONSIDERED something to be trash only to discover it was a priceless treasure to someone else?

During a spring cleaning frenzy, I determined to give away or throw away anything that we didn't use. When I came to our bedroom, I decided I would surprise my husband and clean out his dresser drawers. As I sorted through his belongings, I quickly discovered that a lot of his things were outdated, in need of repair, or too small.

"What are these?" I chuckled as I picked up a tattered pair of black, leather gloves held together by tape. "He can't wear these. I'll buy him a new pair." I tossed them onto the trash pile and continued my cleaning quest.

"What on earth are you doing, Kath?" my husband asked, as he maneuvered through piles on the floor.

"Surprise! I'm cleaning and getting rid of the junk," I announced.

"You're not throwing any of my things away, are you?"

I nodded and pointed to the trash pile.

He plopped down on the floor and began to examine every item. Then he picked up the black leather gloves. He cradled them gently in his hands as if he held a priceless jewel, staring at them for a long time. When he looked at me, his eyes were tear-filled. "These were my dad's."

I froze. I didn't know what to say.

Rich recalled memories of helping his dad with carpentry projects, climbing on the roof with him, and sitting with him in the back of church.

What a relationship they built in only eight short years, I thought, as tears trickled down my cheeks. How sad that I almost trashed something so precious to him. Our journey through grief may not always be understood. Items or memories that appear insignificant and "trash-worthy" to others may be priceless treasures to us. Never underestimate what may trigger your "remembering" tears.

Well-meaning family and friends may think they are helping you get through your loss by removing items from your sight or by unknowingly trashing your treasures. But God is the God of remembrance. He values what was. He understands your loss, your pain, your tears, and your treasure. Trust Him with the memories of your loved one. Tell Him today.

God, I'm crying again, but today it's "remembering" tears. Thank You for giving me memories of my loved one. Thank You for the mementos that trigger memories of a special time. Please help me to forgive the people who have been insensitive to me. They mean well, but they don't understand that what is insignificant to them is priceless to me. You are my God of remembrance. Thank You for understanding and for seeing beyond appearances and looking into my heart. I trust You with my memories. Amen.

My Personal Journey

OTHERS' TEARS

■ ■ ■

Rejoice with those who rejoice; mourn with those who mourn.

ROMANS 12:15

MORE AMERICANS DIED IN the Civil War than in all the other wars combined that the United States was involved in. Approximately 26 percent of the men in the South perished in the struggle, leaving behind a host of grieving parents, wives, and children.

Too often in our journey through grief we forget that others are affected by the loss of our loved one and are suffering too. Family members, young children, coworkers, neighbors, and friends feel deeply, but often we overlook or minimize their pain because we're so absorbed by our own grief. Others may grieve differently than we do, but they still grieve. At times they might even conceal their tears to protect us from pain.

I realized this when my friend Jan came to see me a few months after my son's death. Her constant hugs, acts of kindness, and uplifting attitude were a constant source of encouragement to me during my dark times of sadness and grief, but I never stopped to consider how my son's death had affected her until that day.

Jan's face was somber as she sat down. When I asked her about it, she hesitated. "Kathe, I've been trying to be so strong for you, it never occurred to me I haven't allowed myself to grieve." Jan's lip trembled as a tear trickled down her cheek.

I listened as she shared how my son's death had touched her and her reluctance to tell me since I was enduring my own pain. At that moment I realized that loss impacts others, and I need to give them permission to grieve. Jan and I embraced and cried together.

As you journey through grief, you may encounter others' tears. At times you may need to look beyond your own pain and be sensitive to how others are concealing their grief from you. Hidden grief may be disguised in a mate's silence, a child's misbehavior, or a family member's avoidance or upbeat mood. Remember, you aren't the only one grieving the loss of a loved one. Others may need you to give them permission to share their pain and tears.

Lord, thank You for those who have encouraged me through my loss. Their compassion and sensitivity have strengthened me. Forgive me for the times I've been absorbed in my grief and haven't seen how my loss has affected others. Open my eyes to their hidden grief. Reveal to me who these people are today. Help me to approach them and to comfort them in their grief journey. Amen.

❧

MY PERSONAL JOURNEY

_____

_____

_____

_____

_____

_____

My Personal Journey

GROWING TEARS

I waited patiently for God to help me; then he listened and heard my cry. He lifted me out of the pit of despair, out from the bog and the mire, and set my feet on a hard, firm path and steadied me as I walked along.

PSALM 40:1–2, TLB

AS A CHILD, I used to visit my grandparents' home in the country, where they relied on a cistern to water their garden. The cistern was an artificial reservoir, a rocklike well beneath the ground for storing rainwater. When the autumn rains came, water rushed down the gutters on my grandparents' home and filled the cistern. Then, over the next few months, the water was released to nourish sprouting plants. By summer my grandparents' garden was green and lush, a result of the cistern's life-giving water.

During some seasons in our journey through grief, our reservoir stores up tears, and during other seasons, those tears flow. When we release them, they wash away our anger, guilt, and unforgiveness and water our soul's garden. We feel refreshed and relieved. The seeds of new beginnings and new possibilities begin to take root and emerge from our soul's soil. Tears can nourish us and help us grow through our grief. Over time, we may see a lush, green garden of hope, and our soul might bloom with the strength to press on, a result of God's life-giving power through our tears.

Don't deny yourself or others the opportunity to cry. Too often well-meaning people pat a grieving person on the arm and say, "Oh, don't cry. You'll get through this."

I used to say that to people. Was I uncaring or uncomfortable? No, I believed my words were encouraging. I didn't understand how hurtful they were until I was the receiver of those "comforting" words after my son's death.

Then I realized that storing up my tears wouldn't remove my pain. It only added more emotional debris to my reservoir. I'll never forget the sense of relief I felt when a friend said, "Weep with all your heart. Tears will water and grow your soul." How comforting to have another person recognize that tears are a growing part of my journey through grief.

Maybe that's why Jesus wept after Lazarus died and why Jesus never condemned others for crying, thereby giving us permission to cry as well. Like a cistern, at times our reservoir is full, and we need to release our tears. Give yourself permission to cry in your grief journey. Allow God's power to use your tears to refresh you and transform your soul into a lush garden.

God, crying makes me feel weak and out of control. I don't want others to feel uncomfortable or at a loss for words when I cry, but I do want to be strong again. I know that You wept when You lost loved ones and that You never condemned others for crying. Yet I struggle to give myself permission to cry. Reach down into the cistern of my soul and help me release my fears and tears to You. Wash away my anger, guilt, and unforgiveness. Transform me. Use my tears to water my emerging hopes. Grow my soul into a blooming garden.

My Personal Journey

MY PERSONAL JOURNEY

Section 6 Surrendering

YOUR JOURNEY THROUGH SURRENDERING

Surrendering: *to yield to the power, control, or possession of; to give up completely; to give oneself over to something; to relinquish.*

▪ ▪ ▪

Surrender is the key that unlocks the vault of God's best and deepest treasures.

CHARLES R. SWINDOLL, *INTIMACY WITH THE ALMIGHTY*

Indeed, one step taken in surrender to God is better than a journey across the ocean without it.

Perfectly to will what God wills, to want what He wants, is to have joy; but if one's will is not quite in unison with God's there is no joy.

May God help us to be in tune with Him.

MEISTER ECKHART

JOURNEY INTO THE FIRE OF SURRENDER

For he will be like a refiner's fire or a launderer's soap. He will sit as a refiner and purifier of silver; he will purify the Levites and refine them like gold and silver.

MALACHI 3:2B—3A

THE EMBERS GLOWED AS the blacksmith stoked the fire. One callused hand held a piece of metal to the anvil while the other clasped a hammer. Then he thrust the metal into the fire and pounded. Clang. Thud. Clang. In the fire metal was transformed. The duet of the fire and the hammer continued until the blacksmith's work was finally complete — a masterpiece, a tool.

Loss transforms us, reshaping and redefining who we are. Yet, the refining process isn't anything easy but it sometimes creates terrible pain and discomfort as you place yourself in the divine blacksmith's hands. He pounds his hammer on your anger, then your fears. Another crushing blow upon your blaming and your tears. You're relieved that it's finished, but then you feel the heat. You try to escape, but your fight is futile. Finally you yield to the fire of surrender. The flames melt your pride, guilt, doubt, resentment, and unforgiveness. There's nothing left to melt or pound, you think. You're in the process of being transformed into a masterpiece in the divine blacksmith's hand.

Our journey into the fire of surrender may happen once or numerous times throughout the different seasons of our grief. We discover that it transforms our fear, which becomes faith. Our doubt, which becomes hope. Rather than adopting the identity of widower or childless parent, we forge a new identity as encourager to our family.

Should you decide to enter the fire of surrender and start the process of reshaping, remember that God is the master refiner. He will transform you and your loss into a productive masterpiece.

God, my loss has transformed me. I'm not who I used to be, but I'm confused about who I need to become. I'm afraid to change and move on through my journey of grief. Is now the right time for me? I don't want to resist Your transforming power. Help me yield my loss and my potential to You today. I will enter the fire of surrender and allow You to pound and refine me. You are the master refiner who can remove all the impurities of my grief. Transform my loss and my being into a productive masterpiece that You can use. Amen.

MY PERSONAL JOURNEY

Devotion 27

RUNNING FROM GOD

■ ■ ■

Call upon me in the day of trouble; I will deliver you, and you will honor me.

PSALM 50:15

AT TIMES IN MY grief journey I've resisted God's guidance and direction. My expectations, emotions, or will usually led me astray. But, in spite of my failings and shortcomings, God has always been gracious. Amazingly, He works through me anyway — though, looking back, I wonder how much more of an impact I might have made if I had surrendered to Him instead of running from Him.

Jonah's story gives me hope. He was about as far out of fellowship as a believer can get. He literally was running away from God when that terrifying storm hit his ship and frightened all aboard. Then Jonah confessed his responsibility and convinced the sailors to throw him overboard. Imagine the look of surprise on their sea-soaked faces when the storm stopped. This convinced them of the power of Jonah's God, and they offered a sacrifice to the Lord and made vows to Him. Ironically, God used runaway Jonah to introduce Himself to a shipload of sailors. Unfortunately, Jonah missed out on the celebration and the blessing of seeing his sailing companions experience God as Jonah sank deeper into the sea.

Like Jonah, we may feel as if we are sinking from the burden of our grief. We feel discouraged and distant from God. We begin to think that our grief is our weight to carry and not His. We resist His help, and then we run away. We fool ourselves into believing that we can deal with our sea of personal troubles, sorrows, and consequences. And we may for awhile. We may even sense that we are being used to help others. But in time the waves of our independence are so turbulent they begin affecting others around us. Then we must throw ourselves on God's mercy, believing that He is waiting to save us from our sea of sorrow. Surrendering our grief doesn't mean that we agree with what God plans, but that we acknowledge He knows best and are willing to obey Him anyway.

Surrendering my will, my hurts, and my hopes to God is a daily journey for me. I may still want to run, but that's when God reminds me of Jonah. When Jonah was running from the Lord, God used him to touch a shipload of people. But when Jonah surrendered his life to God, He used him to change an entire city.

Where are you in your relationship with God — in close fellowship or running from Him because you don't understand His purposes — or because you do understand them and don't like them? You cannot escape God. He will pursue you just as He pursued Jonah. Whatever your doubts, pain, anger, or disobedience, God is willing to accept those who call on Him for help. Your past failings, or mine, don't disqualify us from joining God in the great purposes He is working out through our grief even now. What motivation for us to surrender to Him and to be committed fully to do His will. Let's not settle for a shipload of lives to be touched but allow God to use our grief to transform many!

God, I feel disconnected and distant from You. I've allowed my emotions, expectations, and will to lead me astray. I've been running from You. I've resisted Your help and have been trying to carry my burden of grief alone. I'm drowning in discouragement and sorrow. I give up. I'm sorry for running away from You. Please help me throw myself on Your mercy. Save me from my sea of sorrow. I surrender my failings, doubt, pain, anger, and grief to You today. Amen.

My Personal Journey

REQUIRED COURSES

■ ■ ■

May the LORD answer you when you are in distress; may the name of the God of Jacob protect you. May he send you help from the sanctuary and grant you support from Zion. May he remember all your sacrifices and accept your burnt offerings.... May he give you the desire of your heart and make all your plans succeed.

PSALM 20:1—4

MY HIGH SCHOOL AND college diplomas remind me of times when I sat in my advisor's office seeking direction about how to earn my degree and what courses I needed to take. Some courses seemed illogical, yet I suffered through them because I had to in order to reach my goal. Of course, had I been empowered to design the curriculum, I would have chosen electives that required minimal effort.

Our grief journey may feel like being in school again, striving to graduate. We may find ourselves in "required courses" like "Living with Loneliness," "Coping with Change," or "Managing Your Emotions." They are a mandatory part of our grief curriculum. At times we may feel as if we're flunking, with no hope of "graduating" from our grief; while other times we may feel as if we've passed a basic course, only to discover that we're required to take a higher-level class and learn new aspects about grieving.

As a fellow-student in the school of grieving, I've come to realize that my required courses may look different from yours, yet we probably share the same desired outcome — to pass the classes and journey successfully through grief. Numerous times I've been tempted to drop out and wallow in self-pity and bitterness. Although I wanted to succeed, no amount of studying, knowledge, or tutoring was enough to help me pass. I always fell short. That's when I finally gave up trying to do it in my own strength. Surrendering my pain, my loss, and my required courses to God enabled me to persevere.

Although I still haven't graduated from the school of grieving, I know that each required course is one step closer and that my divine advisor is available to encourage me and to remind me to surrender each course to Him.

When I reflect on David's life in 1 and 2 Samuel, I'm reminded of his required courses: "Obedience"; "Success"; "Overcoming Lust, Lying, and Murder"; and "Losing a Son." David understood the outcome of relying on his own strength. He failed many courses, yet his pain and anguish led him to surrender to God.

What about you? What of grief's required courses are you enrolled in? Are you relying on your own strength, or are you ready to surrender your pain and loss to God and to trust God's strength to help you through? He has designed a custom curriculum for you and is ready to be your advisor, to help you journey through grief successfully. Why not let go . . . and let God help?

God, whether I like it or not, I'm a student in the school of grief and I want to learn from You during this time. You know just how tough my courses are and I often feel as if I'm in over my head. Please help me to surrender my grief to You today. Be my divine advisor and encourage me to persevere. Amen.

My Personal Journey

ON THE OTHER SIDE
OF HOWEVER

■ ■ ■

Now faith is being sure of what we hope for and certain of what we do not see.

HEBREWS 11:1

I REMEMBER SITTING IN the front row of the church on the day of our son's memorial service, staring at the teddy bear with three blue balloons on the altar. I had believed God would physically heal our child and had publicly proclaimed His ability to perform a miracle.

But He hadn't.

Months earlier, when I took this stand of faith, I believed God was able to heal our child. However, I predetermined that even if He chose not to, I would praise Him anyway. My journey of faith wasn't an easy one. At times I was flogged with fear, stoned with doubt, chained to expectations, and imprisoned by tears. But God sustained me, guided me safely through, and taught me to surrender. It was a process of letting go of every fear, doubt, expectation, and tear . . . one by one . . . and relinquishing each one to Him. I suffered yet endured.

Facing my son's death and his memorial service was like standing at a crossroads of my faith again, questioning which road to take. The first road was paved, flat, and straight. The alternate route was a dirt and gravel trail. It twisted, turned, and ascended into the mountains.

I prayed and pondered. I wanted to take the smoother road; yet I forged ahead on the dirt and gravel trail toward the mountain. Would the climb be too exhausting? What was on the other side of the mountain? Was I willing to release my fears and doubts and persevere along this trail of surrender to the other side of "however"? Step by step, I trusted God with my pain and discomfort, and He replaced those emotions with a new view of faith.

I'm still in the process of walking up that mountain, but I know, when I finally reach the top, the view will be breathtaking. What I'm most looking forward to is my reward on the other side of the mountain, the other side of however, where my son and God's promises await me.

Many don't understand the concept of delayed reward. Some think that pain is the exception in the Christian life. But we live in a world filled with suffering, even for believers. God is still in control, even if we don't feel like He is. He allows some to experience a trail with much hardship and others to trod on an easier, less painful road.

I'm reminded of this each time I read Faith's Hall of Fame in Hebrews 11. Some mentioned in that hall experienced outstanding victories, even over the threat of death. But others were severely mistreated, tortured, and even killed. All were commended for their faith, yet none of them received what had been promised, their total reward, because they died before Christ came. In God's plan Christians will be rewarded on the other side of however.

While you're on earth, you may never see the purpose of your suffering and loss, but you can be assured that God will keep His promises to you. And He has all of eternity to make it up to you. In times of pain, persecution, or suffering, you may long for an easier route. However, by surrendering each fear, doubt, expectation, and tear to Him, you can stay on the journey of faith and look forward to what the rest of the story will bring . . . on the other side of however.

Where are you on your journey of faith? Are you at the crossroads, longing to take the easier, less painful route? Or are you in the process of trusting God to help you press on in your grief journey to your reward on the other side of however?

Lord, You are trustworthy even when I feel You've let me down. Thank You for sustaining me through my suffering. I want to journey on in my faith. Please help me surrender my fears, doubts, expectations, and tears to You one by one today. I want to trust You beyond what I can see and understand. Refresh my soul with Your hope and promises so that I can journey on to experience all that awaits me on the other side of however. Amen.

MY PERSONAL JOURNEY

_____

_____

_____

_____

_____

_____

_____

_____

_____

_____

_____

_____

_____

_____

Devotion 30

RECEIVING A LIFT
IS A GIFT

■ ■ ■

Therefore encourage one another and build each other up.

1 THESSALONIANS 5:11A

WHO LIFTS YOU UP through your letdowns? Who has tried to support you, though you've refused their help?

Allowing others to encourage us can make us feel uneasy. Somehow it seems easier to give than to receive. If this is true of you, you may be missing out on a healing part of the journey through grief.

Remember the story of the paralytic in Mark's Gospel? Imagine, for a moment, how he must have felt, unable to live life as a healthy man. His eyes filled with tears: *I can't do the things I used to. I don't like being needy.*

The door slammed. He recognized friends' voices. He was surprised they were still speaking to him after his harsh words and insistence that they leave him alone. He felt undeserving of these persistent friends.

The four men gathered around his bed and announced, "We're taking you out today."

His friends dressed him and combed his hair. Although he felt self-conscious, his friends' outpouring of love humbled him. Despite his feelings, he allowed them to place him on the stretcher and carry him through the city. He relaxed and soon joined in with their singing and laughter.

"We're here!" exclaimed his friends as they stopped in front of a house overflowing with people. The paralytic sensed his friends' concern, but before he could speak, they charged up the outdoor steps to the roof, plopped him down, and dug a hole in the roof.

"He's down there!" said his friends as they picked up the man's stretcher and hoisted the paralytic through the hole.

How embarrassing, he thought as his stretcher touched the ground. Silence filled the room. He looked up and saw a man standing beside him. He gazed into the man's soothing and forgiving eyes and felt his discomfort being replaced with calm.

The kind man looked up at the paralytic's friends peering through the hole and then told the paralytic, "Take up your mat and walk!"

Without hesitation, the paralytic responded. He got up and walked.

I've often wondered what would have happened if the paralytic had refused to receive help from his friends?

His life reminds me that surrendering my pride so that I can receive from others is a necessary part of my grief journey. I've learned to accept encouraging words, cards, gifts, prayers, hugs, meals, and help. At times I've felt self-conscious and wanted to resist receiving. That's when God reminded me of a paralyzed man fortunate enough to have compassionate friends who helped him hope again so he could stand up and give again.

Are you in need of a lift? What's keeping you from receiving help? Do you need people to support you? Why not ask God to provide them? Who in your life has lifted you up through your grief journey? Take a moment right now and thank God for each of them.

God, I can feel so paralyzed by my grief. When others try to help me, I push them away. Please help me to surrender my pride to You and allow others to encourage me. Be the healer of my attitude and replace my resistance with assistance. Thank You for the caring people in my life. Lord, use them to lift my soul so that someday I will be able to give again. Amen.

MY PERSONAL JOURNEY

YOUR JOURNEY
THROUGH ACCEPTING

Accepting: *to receive with consent, to give admittance or approval to, to endure without protest, to receive as true, to understand.*

There is only one way to bring peace to the heart, joy to the mind, and beauty to the life. It is to accept and do the will of God.

WILLIAM BARCLAY

There is nothing . . . no circumstance, no trouble, no testing that can ever touch me until, first of all, it has gone past God, and past Christ right through me. If it has come that far, it has come with great purpose, which I may not understand at the moment. But as I refuse to become panicky — as I lift up my eyes to Him to accept it as coming from the throne of God for some great purpose of blessing to my own heart — no sorrow will ever disturb me, no circumstance will cause me to fret, for I shall rest in the joy of what my Lord is that is the rest of victory!

ALAN REDPATH

SEATED AT THE TABLE
OF ACCEPTANCE

■ ■ ■

The kingdom of heaven is like a king who prepared a wedding banquet for his son. He sent his servants to those who had been invited to the banquet to tell them to come, but they refused to come. . . . Then he said to his servants, "The wedding banquet is ready, but those I invited did not deserve to come. Go to the street corners and invite to the banquet anyone you find." So the servants went out into the streets and gathered all the people they could find, both good and bad, and the wedding hall was filled with guests.

MATTHEW 22:2–3, 8–10

"YOUR TABLE IS READY."

I love to hear those words. They assure me that my hungry stomach will soon be satisfied. Most of the time, I don't mind waiting — unless, of course, I see others who arrived after me seated first. It just doesn't seem fair. Though most of us don't long for death the way we long to be seated at a table in a restaurant, it is true that God is preparing a table for us in heaven. But sometimes, others are called before us. A child just opening to life's possibilities, a spouse we don't think we can live without. We may not understand why. It doesn't seem fair. Did God make a mistake? We question, doubt, vent, or cry until nothing else is left to feel. That's usually when we give up and accept the inevitable. In spite of unanswered questions, accepting death is possible.

Your journey to accepting your loved one's death can be as simple as saying, "I give up trying to understand," or "God, I surrender my loved one's death to You."

There is no right way to reach acceptance. Each grief journey is personal. But you will know when you have arrived. You may sense a peace or calm that you never felt before, as if a burden has been lifted so you can smile again. The relief you experience may remind you of how you feel when the hostess announces, "Your table is ready."

God sees the master list, and He understands the purpose and timing of everyone's death. Nothing we can do will change it. What we can do is accept it with His help.

I still struggle to accept my son's death. During times of doubt and despair, I picture the heavenly banquet table that's being adorned with white linen, fine china, crystal, and silver. An endless row of guests waits to be seated. As the divine host calls each name, the person steps forward and is greeted by the Lord, and He shows him or her a reserved seat. After all the guests have arrived and are seated, the Lord sits at the head of the table, and the banquet begins. I envision myself seated at the Table of Acceptance with my son, with Jesus Christ, and with others. What a celebration that will be. I can hardly wait. I hope to see you there!

God, it seems as if I've waited so long for answers to my questions. I know You understand the purpose and timing of my loved one's death even though I don't. Please help me to surrender my uncertainty to You. Replace my despair with peace and my curiosity with calm. Thank You for being Jehovah Shalom, the Lord of Peace. Thank You for being my heavenly host and for preparing a royal banquet table for those who know You. I look forward to dining with You and my loved ones when You call my name and tell me, "Your table is ready." Amen.

My Personal Journey

NEW CLOTHES

■ ■ ■

Therefore, as God's chosen people, holy and dearly loved, clothe yourselves with compassion, kindness, humility, gentleness and patience.

COLOSSIANS 3:12

LOUISE BOUNDED INTO THE kitchen and plopped a brown paper bag on the table.

"Dad, I need to ask you something really important."

Floyd turned slowly from the stove where he was preparing dinner for his family of eight. His role as "chef" was just one of many new roles he was forced to wear since his wife's death.

"I'm all ears . . . but what's in the bag?" Floyd chuckled as he sat down beside Louise and looked into her junior high face. She has her mother's freckles and smile, he thought. Then Louise opened the bag and presented Floyd with a spool of thread, a crumpled pattern, and a wad of fabric.

"I need a new dress for our school concert," she announced. "I know we can't afford to buy one so . . . will you help me make it, Dad?"

Floyd was stunned. He didn't know the first thing about sewing. Thoughts of his former life, when his wife was alive, flooded his mind. He wanted it back but couldn't have it. Here he sat, silently resisting his new reality and his new identity. *Who am I now?* Floyd wondered. *I feel so inadequate as if I've been stripped of my familiar clothes.*

In a sense he had been. God had stripped Floyd of his confidence, life companion, and independence and was in the process of crafting new clothes of dependence, humility, and acceptance. In Floyd's desolate desperation, he cried out to Him and He responded. Miraculously, Louise sported a new dress to the school concert. Although the hemline was a bit uneven, and the buttons didn't match, she wore it proudly because of the loving hands that had crafted it for her.

Floyd's situation reminds me of a scene in the movie *Ivanhoe*. A court jester enters the castle to visit the noble, who is being held prisoner. The noble strips down, clothes himself with the jester's robe, and escapes to freedom disguised as the jester.

Like the noble, your journey through grief may require you to exchange your old clothes for some new ones. Thoughts of your former life may flood your mind. You want your loved one back and things to be the way they were.

You may choose to resist your loss and the roles it forces you to wear and to clothe yourself instead in discouragement, depression, anger, and despair. But you have another choice. You can allow God to strip you and craft new clothes of acceptance. Your new identity may feel as if it doesn't fit at first. At times, you may want to wear the old, familiar clothes, but when you put on compassion, kindness, humility, gentleness, patience, and love you model a new look . . . acceptance of your loss.

How do you see yourself? Wearing the roles and wardrobe of your past? Sporting discouragement, despair, resentment, and resistance? In the process of being stripped down and new clothes and roles being crafted? Or accepting your new identity and wearing a new look?

God, my loss has stripped away my confidence and identity. I wish things were the way they used to be. I don't like the experience of loss and the clothes of discouragement and resistance I've been wearing. Please forgive me. I need You to help me change. Reveal my wrong attitudes, thoughts, and actions and strip them away. Exchange them for a new identity. Help me to accept who I am today and the new roles You have for me to wear. Clothe me with Your compassion, kindness, humility, gentleness, patience, and love so I can reflect You through my loss. Amen.

MY PERSONAL JOURNEY

Devotion 33

LIGHTEN UP!

∎ ∎ ∎

Each one should use whatever gift he has received to serve others, faithfully administering God's grace in its various forms.

1 PETER 4:10

"KATHE, LIGHTEN UP AND have some fun!" The counselor's directive startled me. My blank stare must have tipped her off that fun was a foreign concept for me during this season of grief. If she had suggested I work or encourage others, I could have stepped out with enthusiasm to pursue those goals. But planning fun into my life wasn't my practice or priority. That was evident when she asked me to share what I enjoyed doing, and I struggled to name two things.

Then she instructed me to evaluate the fun people in my life. I listed everyone I interacted with and put a plus or a minus after each person's name to signify if that person energized me (+) or drained me (-).

I was surprised to discover that the majority of people in my life during that season were drainers. They consistently zapped me of energy with their hurtful comments, criticism, expectations, or negative attitudes. Although I valued each relationship, I had nothing left to give at that time.

My counselor asked me to do something extreme — to temporarily cross the drainers off my list and focus my time on the energizers. I resisted. What would the drainers think? Would they feel rejected or disown me? What would God think? Would this be a negative reflection on my faith?

She persisted.

I realized that even Jesus had to take time to withdraw from the needy crowds to rejuvenate. He needed time for fun, laughter, and rest. Did Peter, James, and John fill that role for Him? When He needed a bed-and-breakfast getaway, did Mary, Martha, and Lazarus come to mind? When His cousin John was killed, He recognized that He needed a time away to be silent, to grieve, and to be restored. Jesus kept His life in balance. He gave, but He allowed Himself to receive.

Giving has always come easier for me and seems more spiritually correct than receiving. Yet the Bible tells us that there is a time for everything, and we are to allow others to build us up, and we are to accept their acts of encouragement. My temporary withdrawal from certain people was a necessary step of obedience I needed to take.

But what about those with whom I had to maintain daily contact and couldn't retreat from? In those relationships I set appropriate boundaries and told each person I was unable to give to him or her at that time. Most were understanding and sympathetic, and only a few expressed feelings of rejection and hurt.

That left the energizers on my list. Just the mention of the remaining names encouraged me. They were the type who loved me unconditionally, had no expectations, and made me feel refreshed and renewed. This seemed a little self-indulgent, but I desperately needed to be energized. I unlaced my pride and shared my need for fun and encouragement with them. God used them in a powerful way. Cards, calls, movies, shopping, praying together, a weekend away, and marshmallow fights were unexpected surprises. These special people helped me to lighten up and have fun. They removed my fear of accepting love and attention from others and energized me so I could give again.

Planning fun into my grief journey is now a priority. I often enlist the help of others. When I need to laugh, I call a friend who tells jokes.

When I need a day away, I call my friend who loves to be spontaneous and play. And I'm discovering all the fun things God has created for us to enjoy.

We will always have drainers and energizers in our lives, but when we allow ourselves to give and receive, we can keep our lives in balance. It's good for me to let others know when I need encouragement . . . and then to accept it with a smile!

What about you? Are you balancing your giving and receiving?

Are you in need of receiving encouragement from others?

Do you need to take a break from the drainers and enlist more energizers?

Ask God to show you how to lighten up and accept encouragement from others.

God, why is it that giving is so much easier than receiving? Is my pride preventing me from accepting encouragement from others? I feel empty with nothing to offer right now. I can't give like I used to, and that's hard for me. Help me to evaluate the people in my life and to discern who are drainers and who are energizers. Give me courage to set boundaries with the drainers and share my need to be encouraged with those who energize me. Help me joyfully to accept laughter, fun, and acts of kindness from others. Recharge me with Your healing power and turn my mourning into dancing so I can give again. Amen.

MY PERSONAL JOURNEY

My Personal Journey

A TISSUE AND A CANDLE

■ ■ ■

Your word is a lamp to my feet and a light for my path.

PSALM 119:105

DARKNESS ENCIRCLED HER PATH as she set out for the tomb. *Surely this is a dream,* she thought, wiping a tear from her cheek. *I'll wake up, and my friend will be walking beside me.* But as she recalled the events of the last few days, she knew she wasn't dreaming. Jesus was dead.

Sorrow overwhelmed Mary, and she stumbled on through the blackness. When she reached the tomb's entrance, she gasped. The stone had been moved. *This can't be happening; they've taken my Lord!* she thought. She ran to tell the disciples, then returned to the tomb and stood outside crying.

As she wept, she peered in and saw two angels. "Woman, why are you crying?" they asked.

"They've taken my Lord, and I don't know where they have laid Him," she replied. Then she turned around and saw Jesus standing there but didn't recognize Him. She thought He was the gardener until He spoke.

"Mary." His voice pierced her darkness and illuminated the truth. Mary Magdalene turned toward Him and replied, "Teacher!"

Maybe you're traveling a similar path to Mary's. Your loss feels like a dream, and darkness encircles you. You're stumbling through the blackness, yearning for the stone of disbelief to be rolled away. You want to face the truth, but how can you?

Accepting the truth of your loss and pressing on is a necessary part of your journey through grief. I've discovered that acceptance means more than just facing my loss but also facing the reality that emotions and darkness may be a part of my lifelong quest to deal with my grief. Accepting this about myself has increased my ability to cope.

When others ask how I've survived my loss, I simply reply, "With a tissue and a candle." I accept my emotions and know that I will need a tissue throughout my journey through grief. God is my comforter and the One who wipes my tears.

I also accept the darkness that comes with grief and know that I will need a candle to light my path. God's Word is a consistent light to me. It's a lamp to my feet when I stumble through the darkness. It's God's way of speaking to me. Like Mary, when I hear His familiar voice, I turn around. It pierces the darkness of my grief and illuminates my path with hope.

Are you resisting or accepting where you are? Do you need to face the truth that emotions and darkness may be a continuing part of your journey through grief? Maybe you're in need of a tissue and a candle to help you cope and press on in your journey to acceptance. God's Word will light your path . . . turn to Him today.

God, I've been stumbling through the darkness of my grief, trying to face the truth. I want to journey on to acceptance. I never realized that emotions and darkness could be part of my lifelong quest through grief. Help me accept that today and learn to cope. Comfort me and be a lamp to my feet. When You call to me through Your Word today, help me turn to You. Remove the stone of my despair and replace it with life. Pierce my darkness and illuminate my path with the truth so I can press on. Amen.

"I'LL DO IT"

■ ■ ■

*By faith Abraham, when called to go to a place ... obeyed and went, even
though he did not know where he was going.*

HEBREWS 11:8

WHEN GOD CALLS YOU to do something for Him that doesn't fit your
plans, how do you respond?

A manager overheard someone complaining that a task he had been
assigned didn't suit him. In response to that complaint, the manager said,
"You know, the world's a better place because Michelangelo didn't say,
'I don't do ceilings!'" That comment is worth reflecting on.

Would you agree that the world's a better place because:

A German monk named Martin Luther didn't say, "I don't do doors."
John Wesley didn't say, "I don't do preaching in fields."
Moses didn't say, "I don't do Pharaohs or mass migrations."
Noah didn't say, "I don't do arks or animals."
David didn't say, "I don't do giants."
Mary didn't say, "I don't do virgin births."
Paul didn't say, "I don't do correspondence."
Mary Magdalene didn't say, "I don't do feet."
Jesus didn't say, "I don't do crosses."

And the world will be a better place if you and I don't say, "I don't do ..."

We may miss opportunities to serve God in our journey through grief because we predetermine what we will and won't do without ever consulting Him. Disappointment, fear, denial, or a variety of other excuses can drive us to say, "I don't do grief."

At times I've even said, "I don't do grieving people." I didn't want to be surrounded by people who had lost loved ones, and I certainly didn't want to become labeled as a grief mentor. To my amazement, the more I resisted, the more God persisted. Unwanted opportunities flourished. E-mails, faxes, and phone calls came from people who had lost a loved one and needed encouragement. Complete strangers would stop me and begin to share about their losses. Several friends and family encountered the loss of loved ones, so funerals and sympathy cards became part of my routine. Despite my whining, complaining, bargaining, and blatant refusals, God began to show me that He had a plan for my grief, and I needed to accept it. I finally broke down and told God, "I'll do it."

Little did I know that accepting my loss and the opportunity to be an encourager to those who grieve would change my life. Although grief is still a difficult journey for me, I'm thankful for God's patience as He has guided me through the process. He continues to teach me the necessity of accepting His direction and calling in my life. If He hadn't transformed my "I don't do" thinking into "I'll do it" thinking, you wouldn't be reading this book.

What is God calling you to do in your journey through grief that you've been telling Him, "I don't do"? What steps do you need to take to accept your loss and accept God's plan for using it?

I encourage you to make the world a better place by telling God, "I'll do it!"

God, You've been trying to help me to accept my loss and to use it to help others, but I've resisted and said, "I don't do _____." I've tried denying Your calling, hoping it would go away. I've tried bargaining with You. I've even tried running from You, but You always know just where to find me. The more I resist, the more You persist. I give up! I want to do what-

ever You ask. Thank You for seeing my potential and for accepting me where I am, and thank You for giving me hope by saying "I'll do it" when You died for me on the cross.

MY PERSONAL JOURNEY

My Personal Journey

YOUR JOURNEY THROUGH PRAISING

Praising: *to commend, glorify, worship, value.*

■ ■ ■

Our griefs cannot mar the melody of our praise; they are simply the bass notes of our life song: To God Be the Glory.

C. H. SPURGEON

Praise flourishes as you weed and water and fertilize your spiritual garden in which it grows. It becomes more constant as you nurture your soul on God's Word and walk in His ways, depending upon the Holy Spirit. It gets richer and more spontaneous as you grow in your knowledge of how worthy the Lord is to receive honor and glory and praise.

RUTH MYERS, *31 DAYS OF PRAISE*

To give thanks when you don't feel like it is not hypocrisy; it's obedience.

DR. JOHN G. MITCHELL,
COFOUNDER OF MULTNOMAH SCHOOL OF THE BIBLE

Let everything that has breath praise the LORD.

PSALM 150:6A

THE PATHWAY THROUGH PAIN

■ ■ ■

David noticed that his servants were whispering among themselves and he
realized the child was dead. "Is the child dead?" he asked.
"Yes," they replied, "he is dead."
Then David got up from the ground. After he had washed, put on lotions and
changed his clothes, he went into the house of the LORD and worshiped.

2 SAMUEL 12:19–20A

THE EMPTY CHAIR, THE barren bed, the unworn clothes in the closet, and
the silence — all these remind us will never see our loved one in this lifetime. Our pain feels fresh and sharp again.

King David understood the anguish of grief. Every time he walked
by his son's room he must have sensed death's presence. What would life
be like without his child? No more laughter. No tucking him in at night.
No birthdays, no heir to his throne.

David had pleaded for God to spare his child. But his son had died.

Then David's pain drove him to God. He knew he needed to be in
God's presence after his son's death. Remarkably, David recognized that
the pathway through pain was praise.

Praise focuses on who God is and on His nature, character, and
power. Like David, when we think of who God is or of something He
has done, our hearts overflow with gratefulness. It's all right if our praise
emerges in the midst of our pain. Joyful praise isn't necessarily more
valuable to God. He doesn't enjoy our praise on the basis of how warm
and happy we feel but on the condition of our hearts.

As C. S. Lewis has said, we may honor God more in our low times than in our peak times. We may bring Him special joy when we find our-selves depressed or wiped out emotionally. We may look around at a world from which God seems to have vanished and still choose to trust Him and praise Him in spite of how we feel.

Praise brings the refreshment of God's presence into our situation. It helps us view our loss through different lenses by focusing on God rather than our circumstances. Often this change of vision transforms the atmosphere around us. In turn, a new attitude causes people to react differently to us, and we begin to exert a creative and uplifting influence on others.

As we fill our lives with praise, God will reveal Himself to us in new ways. He'll also reveal Himself through us to others.

Who is God to you? What has He done for you? Praise Him!

God, I praise You for being my faithful Father. You're always there, ready to hold me. You are my Comforter, the One who wipes away my tears. I praise You for being my companion through the journey of grief. You are the Healer of my broken heart. When I focus my attention on You and not on my circumstance, my pain lessens. Help me to continue to praise my way through the pathway of pain. Amen.

MY PERSONAL JOURNEY

My Personal Journey

MOUNTAIN MOVER

■ ■ ■

LORD, you have been our dwelling place throughout all generations. Before the mountains were born or you brought forth the earth and the world, from ever-lasting to everlasting you are God.

PSALM 90:1–2

"KATHE, WE'VE DECIDED TO give you a Labor of Love shower," my friends announced.

I was stunned. I thought: *Most women would be thrilled to be showered with baby gifts, but when your baby is expected to die, a shower is just one more painful reminder of your loss.*

"We know your situation is unique, but you deserve to be encouraged," my friends explained. "We'd like to give you an uplifting day of singing, prayer, food, and surprises."

I was touched. Even though it seemed a bit odd, I sensed God smiling at the whole idea. I began to look forward to my Labor of Love shower and to the support and encouragement I would receive, even if it was packaged in an untraditional way.

The day of the shower, when I entered the family room, I was amazed to see nearly fifty women amidst the streamers and balloons. A "Labor of Love" banner with personalized comments adorned the wall. The outpouring of love and encouragement was overwhelming.

My friend Ginger touched my arm. "It's really hard for me to be here today," she tearfully replied. "I almost didn't come."

I gave her a reassuring hug and thanked her for attending. As if on cue to break the tension, a woman handed us song sheets and directed us to our seats as a symphony of singing voices filled the air.

While the last chorus was sung, I waddled to the center of the room and plopped down in a designated chair. Caring eyes flooded my vision. I suspected many women had hidden questions. How was I coping with the pending loss of my baby? Did I feel angry or afraid? What was God teaching me through this experience? Did I believe God would perform a miracle?

During the past several months, I had lived with the painful prognosis that death was imminent for my baby. Yet I clung to the hope that God would perform a physical miracle. This conviction led me on a lonely journey during which I felt misunderstood by others. Most believed I was in denial and unable to face reality. I was convinced that my stand of faith was how God wanted me to respond. I endured silent ridicule, questioning stares, and thoughtless comments. At times I chose to isolate myself from others so I wouldn't be tempted to waver in my belief that God would heal my child.

God, please give me the right words to say, I prayed now as I sat surrounded by women waiting for me to speak.

Over the next few moments I recalled the bittersweet journey of my surprise pregnancy after fifteen years of marriage, infertility, and adoption. I shared how I enjoyed carrying my unborn child and believed that God was able to heal our baby, but that even if He chose not to, I would still trust Him. The words that I blurted out next surprised me. "We all face mountains in our life journey. They block our view, they paralyze us with fear and hopelessness, they stand as a monument of what we can't control. But the pathway to faith and victory is to focus on the Mountain Mover and not on the mountain."

Tears stung my eyes as I pondered these words and remembered the many personal mountains God had moved in this roomful of friends.

At that point Ginger left the room. Moments later I saw her maneuvering through the crowd toward me. She smiled and handed me a soft, gray bundle. "Kathe, I had to give you this after I heard you speak. It's been in the trunk of my car for several months. Now I know why I never took it out."

I looked at the ordinary gray T-shirt. Slowly, I unrolled it. When I saw its inscription, I gasped. "Mountain Movers . . . faith that moves mountains. Matthew 17:20," it read.

God affirmed me in a powerful, visual way that day. "Mountain Movers" became my labor and delivery motto. I even ordered T-shirts so my friends could sport the Mountain Movers motto when they came to the hospital during my delivery. But God surprised us all when a man in the waiting room asked whether they knew Ginger. He explained that he had created the Mountain Mover T-shirts for her. I could almost hear God chuckling and saying, "If I can orchestrate it so the man who created your T-shirt is at the hospital during your delivery, don't you think that I, the Creator of the universe, the Almighty Mountain Mover, am surely with you?"

My long night of labor was difficult, but I kept focusing on the T-shirt hanging on my hospital wall. God was faithful to the motto He had given me. He moved my mountain of fear and replaced it with faith. He used my situation to soften hospital workers' hearts, moving them closer to Himself. He moved multitudes across the country to pray for us. And even though my son didn't survive, God gave me the privilege of being his mother and the faith to believe I will see him again in heaven.

What about you? What mountain are you facing today that blocks your view? I encourage you to focus not on your mountain of grief but on the only one strong enough to move it. Then praise Him for His faithfulness.

God, I praise You for being bigger than the mountain I'm facing today. I'm sorry that I've allowed it to obstruct my view of You. Help me to trust You. Help me to believe You. Replace my fear with faith. Please help me to fix my eyes on Your almighty power and faithfulness today. Remind me of the many mountains that You have already moved in my life. Thank You for being my Mountain Mover today. Amen.

MY PERSONAL JOURNEY

_____

_____

_____

_____

_____

_____

_____

_____

_____

_____

_____

_____

_____

_____

_____

_____

_____

_____

_____

_____

_____

_____

_____

Devotion 38

PAIN PRODUCING PRAISE

■ ■ ■

Praise be to the name of God for ever and ever; wisdom and power are his. He changes times and seasons; he sets up kings and deposes them. He gives wisdom to the wise and knowledge to the discerning. He reveals deep and hidden things; he knows what lies in darkness, and light dwells with him. I thank and praise you, O God of my fathers.

DANIEL 2:20–23A

PAIN OFTEN PRODUCES SOMETHING of great value. I'm reminded of that every time I see a pearl. Oddly, the priceless pearl began as a pebble or particle of sand within an oyster's shell. This painful irritant prompted the oyster to secrete a calcium-like substance that hardened into smooth, concentric circles around the object. When the oysters are harvested and their shells are pried open, often you'll discover a valuable gem ... the product of their pain.

That's how I feel about losing a loved one. Our pain can often produce something of great value. During my own grief journey, the book *31 Days of Praise* became a priceless gem to me. It pointed me to a new understanding of praising God in the midst of my pain.

I always had believed that praising was synonymous with smiles, happiness, and enthusiasm ... not something that could encompass tears and pain. Now I realize praising allows us to rely on God and focus on His character and attributes in spite of our pain.

Oddly, the gem of a book that soothed my soul began when a young wife sojourned in Taiwan, the Philippines, and Hong Kong during her first husband's intense suffering with cancer before the Lord called him home. During her years as a widow with two young children, her book was born. It flowed out of truths that had long motivated her to trust and worship the Lord in the varied seasons and experiences of life. I'm grateful to Ruth Myers for allowing God to transform her painful irritant of loss into a product of great value that has touched my life and that of many others as well.

When you reflect on your loss and the pain it inflicts, remember that pain can prompt you to call out to God in praise. Praise isn't denying the pain but pronouncing who God is in the midst of your pain. Praise is a priceless gem that you can discover today. Allow your pain to produce praise.

Almighty God, author of life and death, You are compassionate and understanding. You accept me today where I am and love me. You are my hope-giver, my encourager, my friend. Praising You doesn't come easily for me because my life is so painful. Use my pain to prompt me to praise You. Transform my irritant of loss into the priceless gem of knowing You in a deeper way. Amen.

My Personal Journey

_____

_____

_____

_____

_____

_____

_____

_____

My Personal Journey

DEEP ROOTS

■ ■ ■

But blessed is the man who trusts in the LORD, whose confidence is in him. He
will be like a tree planted by the water that sends out its roots by the stream.
It does not fear when heat comes; its leaves are always green. It has no worries
in a year of drought and never fails to bear fruit.

JEREMIAH 17:7–8

A STORM RAVAGED MY neighborhood. Broken tree limbs cluttered the streets, and uprooted tree trunks blanketed the lawns. But some trees stood unharmed from the ferocious wind. How had they survived the storm?

I realized that a tree's strength is hidden beneath the surface, in its roots. The deeper the roots, the stronger the tree. The trees with deep roots were anchored securely and endured the storm, unlike their shallow-rooted friends.

When the storms of grief rage through my life, am I ripped apart or do I persevere? What keeps me anchored and standing tall?

As I took inventory of my varied responses during my grief journey, I realized that my strength came from being rooted in God's presence. When I focus on who God is, I am able to stand. When I choose to see God as the light in the midst of my darkness, or my rock in the midst of my crumbling emotions, or my shield when I feel as if I'm being hit with arrows of doubt and discouragement, I can cope with grief. But when I take my eyes off Him and focus on myself or my situation, I feel uprooted.

I've decided to stay rooted in praising God. When the winds of loneliness try to blow me over, I see God as my companion. When the hail of despair pounds at my door, I welcome God in as my hope. If the freezing rain of fear begins to creep into my soul, I cry out to God as my warm encourager. Whatever I sense my greatest need is at the time, one of God's characteristics counterbalances it.

Whether we choose to acknowledge Him or not, He is our root of security. It's up to us how we choose to respond.

Jeremiah encourages us to grow deep spiritual roots and respond to our circumstances by trusting God. By the world's standards, Jeremiah was a failure. For forty years he served as God's spokesman, but nobody listened. He was rejected, ignored, mistreated, and alone much of his life. Yet he survived by looking beyond his circumstances with faith and courage to God.

When we choose to be rooted in God's presence and to focus on Him, we can be assured that no matter what takes place we can rely on His wisdom, goodness, mercy, and truth. Like Jeremiah, we can have deep spiritual roots that will enable us to endure the storms of grief.

What storms are you facing?

Do you feel ripped apart and broken, or are you standing tall?

You can weather any circumstance by being rooted in God's presence.

God, thank You for being with me through my storms of grief. You've been my Comforter when I cried, my Strength when I was weak, my Sight when I couldn't see past my circumstances, my Light in the dark night of my soul. Forgive me for the times I didn't acknowledge Your presence. I know You never left me. Reveal Yourself to me in every situation I face, and help me to stay rooted in You. Amen.

My Personal Journey

JOURNEY TO THE
SCHOOLHOUSE OF PRAISE

■ ■ ■

Praise the LORD, O my soul; all my inmost being, praise his holy name.

PSALM 103:1

DOWN A DUSTY, GRAVEL road in the middle of nowhere stands a little country schoolhouse nestled between a grove of pine trees and a church cemetery with a white picket fence. A woman clad in a dark, floor-length dress emerges from the schoolhouse and clangs a bell. Children scurry up the rickety wooden steps and file one by one through the doorway to take their familiar seats. The room is divided into two sections: larger desks on one side for the older children and smaller desks on the other for the younger ones.

In the back corner stands a makeshift sink: an orange crate turned on its end with a wash pan filled with water atop it. In the other corner is the coatrack and a shelf filled with lunch pails. The aroma of books and wood fills the air along with a hint of smoke from the wood-burning stove. As is her habit, the teacher shares Scripture and prayer and then walks behind her desk to the front wall.

All eyes peer at her hand as she picks up the chalk and begins to print on the blackboard: A ... B ... C ... She continues until Z and then turns to face the class. "Today's lesson will be to focus on words that start with each letter of the alphabet," she announces.

One by one the children take turns walking to the blackboard to scribble a word for their assigned letter. Words like apple, butterfly, cat, dog, frog, and snake adorn the blackboard.

The teacher nods and continues, "Class, now I want you to take out a sheet of paper and write down your own personal words for each letter. Think about things you enjoy, things that are special to you."

The teacher collects the papers and begins to review them at her desk. She is amazed to discover the variety of words the students have written to express what each letter means to them personally. A-art, A-acorn-picking, A-August, A-automobiles, A-azaleas, A-Ann. She realizes an important truth: Though the letters are constant and the same, what they represent is different.

Praising our way through grieving is much like this one-room schoolhouse scene. We all have something in common, yet may be at different stages of our learning. But the one constant we can count on is God. As we write the ABCs of who God is on the blackboard of our souls, the words we each choose to describe Him are personal. Go ahead, try it. Write a word for each letter to describe who God is to you. And when you've finished, tell Him. He will love to receive your ABCs of praise.

God, I acknowledge You as my teacher. Sometimes I feel like a slow learner when it comes to praising You through my pain. I understand that grief is a required course for me, and I'm in the process of learning more about it. Praise is another. I know I'm not alone in this classroom of learning. You stand at the front of the classroom and point me to the spiritual blackboard. "Who am I to you?" You ask. "Tell me today."

I will, Lord. You are . . .

A

B

C

D

E

F

G

H

I

J

K

L

M

N

O

P

Q

R

S

T

U

V

W

X

Y

Z

Amen.

My Personal Journey

My Personal Journey

YOUR JOURNEY
THROUGH BEING

Being: *the quality or state of having existence, life, essence, personality, presence, reality, actuality; to endure; to dwell.*

If the pace and the push, the noise and the crowds are getting to you, it's time to stop the nonsense and find a place of solace to refresh your spirit.

CHARLES R. SWINDOLL, *INTIMACY WITH THE ALMIGHTY*

How rare it is to find a soul quiet enough to hear God speak.

FRANÇOIS FÉNELON

Be still, and know that I am God.

PSALM 46:10

BEING WITH THE SHEPHERD

■ ■ ■

The LORD is my shepherd, I shall not be in want. He makes me lie down in green pastures, he leads me beside quiet waters, he restores my soul. He guides me in paths of righteousness for his name's sake. Even though I walk through the valley of the shadow of death, I will fear no evil, for you are with me; your rod and your staff, they comfort me.

PSALM 23:1—4

THE FUNERAL WAS OVER, the crowd was gone, and the tension of the past few days had diminished. I had no more tears to cry. Exhausted, I felt hollow and alone. How do I begin to heal? How do I get back to normal?

Silence penetrated our home. Usually I would have welcomed it, but instead of soothing me, it made me feel awkward. I was relieved when the doorbell rang.

A stranger stood at my door, carrying a tray of food. She smiled and explained that she had prepared a meal for our family. When I invited her in, she brushed by me, headed for the kitchen, and began to unpack.

"Enjoy your dinner," she said and turned to leave. "You can expect others to bring meals for the next two weeks."

I was touched that so many people would volunteer to cook dinner for us. How humbling to think that in such a busy, demanding world, others had found time to be used by God to provide for me.

Over the next couple of weeks, I began to experience "being" in a new way. I used to equate being with silence and rest, but I began to realize that the state of being encompassed much more than this. Being is the very essence of who we are ... being in need, being available, being servants, and being served. I realized that being weak, tired, and in need were okay. Those conditions allowed God to use others as providers.

Little did I know that being served by others for the next couple of weeks would also give me another unexpected gift: time to focus on being with God. Instead of cooking, I used my time to pray, journal, read the Bible, and listen to God. During that time, God allowed me to relate to Him as my shepherd, and He encouraged me through Psalm 23. I realized that God had provided a season of being for me to rest, to be restored, and to be provided for. He took care of daily needs and enabled me to be physically and spiritually nourished. And He showed me the importance of being with Him during my journey through grief.

Being with the Shepherd now forms a necessary part of every day. Some days I set my dining room table for two and invite God to be with me for breakfast as I read His Word. Other days I schedule time with Him in my backyard, at the bagel shop, or behind closed doors at my office to sit in silence and just listen.

A few times throughout the year I schedule a DAWG Day (Day Alone with God). Whether I check into a hotel, take a drive out of town, go to a park, or spend the day at the cemetery, I spend time with God and allow Him to be the Shepherd who restores me. In turn, I ask Him to reveal ways I can be available to others to pass on the gift of "being" with Him.

Never underestimate the eternal value of preparing a meal for someone. Like me, others might find they've been given the unexpected gift of time to be with the Shepherd. That, after all, is the greatest gift a grieving person can have.

> *God, You are my Shepherd, the provider and the restorer of my soul. Thank You for prompting people to be available and to serve. Thank You for the times when I'm in need and for meeting those needs in unexpected ways. Thank You for being with me in my journey through grief. Help me to make being with You a priority, a noncancelable appointment that I look forward to. Restore me during those times and show me ways that I can encourage others to be with You. Amen.*

MY PERSONAL JOURNEY

Devotion 42

BEING IN THE DARKNESS

■ ■ ■

You, O LORD, keep my lamp burning; my God turns my darkness into light.

PSALM 18:28

WHEN I WAS A child, I used to dread walking into my dark bedroom. I would stand at my doorway and peer into the unlit room, which seemed eerie and uninviting. My imagination ran wild with thoughts of what might lurk in my closet or beneath my bed. Frequently I bargained with my parents and made excuses to postpone bedtime. Eventually I had no choice but to face my fear and enter the darkness.

Loss leads to darkness. Darkness comes no matter how hard we try to avoid it. However threatening it might appear, eventually we must face it and enter it alone.

Darkness descended on me several months after my son's death. For the first few weeks I was inundated with phone calls, letters, and visitors. I quickly returned to work and filled my calendar with activity. People and organizations sought me out to share about my loss. In addition to my work, speaking, and being a wife and mother, I assumed additional community leadership roles. I didn't realize that darkness loomed ahead and that all my activity was only postponing it.

When I discovered I was pregnant again, I was thrilled. I believed God was healing my hurt. But then I miscarried our baby. I was devastated and couldn't believe I was facing another loss so soon.

Then I woke up one morning and didn't want to get out of bed. At that moment I felt myself slipping into a dark cave of despair and dread. I had no motivation or desire to be around people. When others spoke to me, I had difficulty hearing what they were saying. Never had I experienced such emptiness, anguish, and aloneness. Would I live in darkness forever?

A few days later I read that the quickest way to reach the light of day isn't to run west toward the setting sun, which seems natural, but to do the opposite. Head east and enter the darkness until you come to the sunrise. At that moment I knew that my darkness was unavoidable. I could try to outrun it or postpone it, but eventually I would have to walk into the darkness of my loss to be transformed.

I made a decision to journey into darkness, to yield to my pain and loss. When I gave myself permission to grieve wherever or whenever, intentionally or spontaneously, I was surprised how free I felt and how inoffensive my decision was to others. It actually encouraged others to mourn their loss as well.

I scheduled time in my life for solitude so I could be in the darkness alone. Sometimes I slipped away to my bedroom and listened to music, mostly instrumentals or praise-worship tapes; sometimes I took a bath and read a book; at other times I went for a drive. Mostly, I curled up on my couch late at night and stared into the darkness, reliving my loss and what could have been.

Praying was hard for me. Sometimes all I could do was groan or mumble a few words to tell the Holy Spirit to pray on my behalf. This gave God an opportunity to draw near to me.

The regular ritual of being in the darkness was painful but productive. It became sacred to me, and my spirit yearned for this authentic time of grieving my loss. Being in the darkness enlarged my soul. I didn't get over my loss, but I learned to live with it. I sensed God's comfort. The light of His love illuminated the dark places in my heart, and both darkness and light helped to transform me.

Darkness is a continuous part of my journey through grief. It is not a one-time experience but is a constant companion to me as over time I discover new dimensions of my loss. Unlike my childhood, being in the dark isn't something I dread or fear now, but a place I willingly enter into, a place where God can draw near and change me.

What about you? Are you afraid of the dark? Have you been running from it and postponing your entry into it? Or have you plunged into the night-depths of your soul to be transformed by the experience?

You can't escape it, so stop trying. Go ahead, enter the darkness. And remember, you won't be alone. God is your comforter, intercessor, and light. His love will see you through and enlarge your soul.

God, darkness is closing in on me. I've been trying to avoid the inevitable and need You to help me realize that being in the darkness is part of my journey through grief. I don't want to dread or fear it but to embrace it and allow You to use it to change me. Slow me down, Lord, and allow me to face my pain and loss. Be my comforter, encourager, companion, and light. Illuminate the dark night. Show me today how being in the darkness has and will enlarge my soul. Amen.

MY PERSONAL JOURNEY

My Personal Journey

SLOW DOWN AND DETOUR
TO THE SCHOOL OF BEING

Come to me, all you who are weary and burdened, and I will give you rest.

MATTHEW 11:28

As RICH HANDED ME an envelope, I could tell by my husband's anxious look that something important was inside. Curiosity and excitement gripped me. *Maybe it's an unexpected check or a letter announcing I've won a contest,* I thought. I ripped open the envelope to claim my treasure, only to find an official-looking document with my picture on it.

To my disappointment and surprise I discovered that my "treasure" was a photo radar traffic ticket. I had been caught speeding. *It must be a mistake,* I thought. However, the snapshot of a woman behind the wheel driving my vehicle with my license plate proved I was guilty. My violation read, "Speed greater than reasonable and prudent."

I considered my options: Pay the fine, contest the citation by appearing in court, or attend a defensive driving school. We agreed I should go to school.

"My life is so hectic, how can I fit two nights of class into my schedule?" I whined.

Rich gazed deep into my eyes. "Maybe it's time you slowed down, Kath."

His words hit a nerve. *Maybe he's right,* I thought. *Why do I have this compelling need to jam my schedule with activity?* As I pondered this question,

I realized that since my son's death, work and busyness had been my constant companions. In some strange way, they comforted me. I equated activity with productivity. Yet, as I examined my lifestyle, I could see that I was in the speed trap of grief . . . going too fast to feel the pain of my loss. The speed of my activity was greater than reasonable and prudent, and I needed to slow down.

That scared me. I liked the fast pace, and slowing down would force me to focus on the road signs of my loss. The idea felt uncomfortable and inconvenient — like a road under construction, filled with bumps, holes, and dirt.

Martha understood this all too well; yet she struggled with lessening her load of activity. She loved multitasking and could accomplish more in one day than most people she knew. She thrived on noise and "doing," unlike her sister, Mary, who could ignore her work and spend hours reading, reflecting, or listening to a friend.

What a waste of productive time, Martha thought as she glared at her sister, sitting contently at their guest's feet. *I'm doing all the work, and she's doing nothing!* Martha's anger flared. *It's time Mary picked up the pace and got busy!*

Martha stormed into the room and demanded that Jesus settle the matter and instruct her sister to help her. To Martha's surprise, he gazed into her eyes and gently replied, "Martha, Martha, . . . you are worried and upset about many things, but only one thing is needed. Mary has chosen what is better, and it will not be taken away from her" (Luke 10:41).

These words hit a nerve in Martha. *Maybe he's right,* she may have thought. *Why do I have this compelling need to stay busy?* Martha pondered this question, perhaps realizing she felt uneasy when she slowed down. It forced her to be alone with herself, her thoughts, her questions and fears, and with God. That scared her. Yet, when she looked at Mary, her soul yearned to slow down and readjust her pace and her priorities. She knew this was a necessary part of her journey.

Filling your life with too much activity can prevent growth and healing in your journey through grief. Sooner or later you will get caught in the speed trap of grief and be forced to realize that you are driving yourself at a speed that is neither reasonable nor prudent. It's time to slow down! You can't pay off this offense with money, and the longer you contest it, the longer you prolong your restoration.

Clearly, the best solution is to become a student in the school of being. It may be hard for you to readjust your pace and your priorities. It may feel uncomfortable to be alone with yourself, your thoughts, your questions and fears, and with God. Like Martha, you need to slow down and take the detour to the school of being. It's a necessary part of your journey.

God, my life is hectic and speeding out of control. Busyness and work have been my companions since my loss. They comfort me and distract me. I'm afraid to slow down and be alone with myself and with You. I've been filling the void with activity. Please forgive me. I want to readjust my pace and my priorities and allow You to help me to grow and heal. Be the radar to my soul and slow me down, Lord. Help me to take this detour and become a student in the school of being. Amen.

MY PERSONAL JOURNEY

My Personal Journey

JOURNEY TO THE
COCOON OF BEING

■ ■ ■

Then I prayed to Jehovah. "Lord," I pled, "you are my only place of refuge.
Only you can keep me safe."

PSALM 142:5, TLB

THE PROCESS OF ADAPTING to loss and change takes energy. Grief can
be draining, causing us to feel more tired and irritable than usual. In
turn, our ability to focus and function in other areas of our lives may be
lessened. And we may want to isolate ourselves from others, to hide in
the safety of our homes.

When we're going through grief, we need to be gentle with ourselves.
We don't have to measure up to who we normally are and what we usually can deliver. Giving ourselves permission to lighten our load, to do
less and to be more, is healthy and essential. We're changing. Our physical and emotional needs may be different now, requiring us to welcome
more rest, quiet, and comfort from others. We may be more needy. We
may find it necessary to remove ourselves from activity for a season and
enter a time of solitude. Our grief journey may lead us to a place where
we need to cocoon ourselves so we can be transformed.

God reminded me of this when I saw a caterpillar, who was ugly, vulnerable, and welcome prey to any bird in the neighborhood. How will it
survive? I wondered. Then I realized that a caterpillar instinctively
forms a silklike envelope around itself during a specific time in its journey. It ceases crawling on leaves and enters a state of just "being." The

cocoon is the caterpillar's new home. It protects it from predators and the environment. It provides a safe place. During this season of being, the caterpillar undergoes change. Then one day it emerges from the cocoon, transformed into a butterfly. It has new energy and a different purpose. It has wings to fly. And it does.

Like the caterpillar, we may experience seasons in our journey through grief when we must just "be" to survive and to be transformed. We may have to relinquish expectations, activity, and responsibilities during this time. We may enter our cocoon feeling ugly, vulnerable, and prey to people's insensitivity and our own expectations. How will we survive apart from others? we ponder. But we can. We are never alone, for God, our Transformer, is with us.

When we choose to leave our expectations and activity behind and enter the state of being, we undergo change. Rest and solitude comfort us. God speaks to us in our stillness, and we gain new insights about our loss. We learn the value of loving and caring for ourselves. We feel safe in God's arms and surrender to Him as He transforms the ugliness of our grief into something beautiful.

In time, we emerge from our cocoon of being, transformed into a new creature and excited about life again. We have new energy and an enlarged perspective about our loss. Before long, we take wing and fly!

God, I'm drained and exhausted from my loss. I feel as if I have nothing to give. It's hard to cope, and I don't know how to change. I know that I'm needy right now. Help me accept that about myself. Give me the strength to step away from expectations and activity for a season and cocoon myself so I can be renewed and restored. Wrap Your loving arms around me and change me. Transform the ugliness of my grief into something beautiful so that in time I can take wing and fly. Amen.

My Personal Journey

ENJOY THE NOW

■ ■ ■

Don't be anxious about tomorrow. God will take care of your tomorrow too.
Live one day at a time.

MATTHEW 6:34, TLB

WHEN MY FRIEND LISA and I planned our annual getaway, we were expecting a stress-free, pampered weekend with no responsibilities, no schedules, and limitless conversation. But we soon discovered that our luxurious bed-and-breakfast was a dark, musty apartment cluttered with cobwebs and mismatched furniture. The "gourmet" breakfast that the brochure acclaimed was handed to us in a box when we checked in, and we were told to refrigerate it until morning.

My discontent and frustration ignited as I remembered our past getaways. Visualizing the multitude of better accommodations we had experienced and could be experiencing, I became more critical of the present situation. I longed for what had been and what could possibly be. I didn't want to be in this moment. I wanted out!

Fortunately, God is faithful to guide us back on the path of right thinking when we go astray. He used Lisa's gentle spirit, humor, and words to help me see that I was allowing the past and the future to rob me of the present. Lisa chose to make the most of our experience, to seize the day and the moment. I, on the other hand, almost missed out on fun with a friend.

The time for doing and living is now. Too often in our journey through grief our todays slip by unnoticed because we are so preoccupied with tomorrow or absorbed with yesterday that we miss the here and now.

Our journey through grief may take us to an unexpected fork in the road with two road signs: "What Was" and "What Will Be." Then we notice the third sign: "What Is." At first we didn't see it because we were so distracted by the other two. Which way do we allow our grief to take us? If we don't live in the now, we may be destroying our future. For it is the present that shapes the future.

I've learned to ask God, "Show me what's on Your agenda for me today and help me to make the most of the present." He may reveal a friend in need of encouragement, a verse to pray for my husband, or an inspiring idea for an article. Or God may remind me to simply embrace the present moment in silence, sensing His presence in the wind, the rain, or the sun.

God encourages us to enjoy the now. He calls himself "I Am," not "I Was" or "I Will Be." Like Lot's wife, who looked back to her past and was turned to salt, ignoring today and focusing on what life was like before our loved one died can have lasting consequences. We may miss out on moments that we will never be able to recapture . . . today's sunset, our child's hug, or a conversation with God. Although God does give goals and promises for the future, His focus is on the present. He is the God of the now.

What past regrets or future worries are robbing you of enjoying your present? Maybe it's time to release them to God and refocus your thinking on enjoying the now.

God, I can see how the road signs of "What Was" and "What Will Be" can distract me from enjoying "What Is." Please help me to release my regrets and worries to You today. Forgive me for missing moments with others and with You. Help me to enjoy being and living in the present and show me how to maximize my moments. Thank You for being "I Am," the God of the now. Amen.

My Personal Journey

My Personal Journey

Your Journey Through Celebrating

Celebrating: *to honor, memorialize, dedicate, keep; to demonstrate satisfaction by festivities or other deviation from routine; to hold up for public acclaim; to observe a holiday; to observe a notable occasion with festivities.*

What the heart has once known,
It shall never forget.

AUTHOR UNKNOWN

What was hard to bear is sweet to remember.

PORTUGUESE PROVERB

Death is not a period bringing the sentence of life to a
close
Like the spilling of a moment or the dissolution of an
hour.
Death is a useful comma
Which punctuates, and labors to convince
Of more to follow.

WILLIAM WALTER DeBOLT

Devotion 46

CELEBRATE YOUR
FRAMED MEMORIES

■ ■ ■

*Be joyful always; pray continually; give thanks in all circumstances, for this
is God's will for you in Christ Jesus. . . . Test everything. Hold on to the good.*

1 THESSALONIANS 5:16—18, 21

BIRTHDAYS. ANNIVERSARIES. SPECIAL OCCASIONS. Holidays. They still
come. But they are different now. Some who grieve choose to ignore
them while others choose to celebrate them. Our response may change
from year to year. Grief is a personal journey that allows each of us to
celebrate our memories and to remember our loved ones in our own way
and in our own time.

After my friend Margie lost her teenage son Danny in an accident,
she told me she dreaded holidays. In the past, holidays had been a time
when her entire family gathered to celebrate, and Danny was usually the
center of attention. Family pictures were a traditional part of their time
together, and trying to come up with creative shots was part of their fun,
always with the aim of outdoing the last family photograph. The family
pictures displayed throughout Margie's home represented so many
memories.

She chuckled as she recalled the year they dressed formally. "Danny
must have been about three, and I had to buy him a suit just like the
men. He looked so cute!" Margie's eyes misted with tears as she smiled.
"I was in such a hurry to get everyone dressed that I forgot his underwear.

I can still hear Danny's shrill little voice reminding me what I forgot when I tried to zip his pants!"

Framed memories. Forever in our hearts. We may move the photos out of sight, but they are never out of mind.

Margie and her family decided to celebrate their personal memory of Danny in a family photograph Christmas card. They chose California sand, blue sky, and endless ocean as the backdrop because Danny loved the beach. Jagged rocks were used as the chairs. The family dressed casually, but what each person wore was special. Her husband and son-in-law wore Danny's favorite shoes. Her daughters wore jewelry Danny had given them. Another son-in-law sported Danny's favorite T-shirt. Margie's grandchildren tucked Danny's Legos in their pockets. And Margie held Danny's framed picture next to her heart.

Celebrating the memory of our loved ones is personal. Margie's family celebrated through a photograph. It may be different for you. You may choose a quiet visit to the cemetery, starting a scholarship fund in your loved one's name, or sharing your loved one's prized possessions with others.

Remembering our loved ones in special ways can be exhausting or exhilarating. When you look at your framed snapshots of memories, what do you see?

Let's remember . . . not to forget.

Gracious God, special events force me to face the memories of my loved one. I don't want to forget him (her), but sometimes it hurts to go through another special occasion without him (her). Help me to remember the good. Use me to create something special as a memorial to my loved one's life. I want to frame his (her) memories and celebrate. Amen.

My Personal Journey

THE MEMORY BOX

━━━ ■ ■ ■ ━━━

I thank my God every time I remember you.

PHILIPPIANS 1:3

MEMORIES ARE A PRICELESS treasure. They keep our loved ones close to us. But when we open the lid to our box of memories, we never know what to expect. Recalling the past might evoke laughter, tears, hope, or fears. Each season of our grief journey is different. Specific occasions may trigger our need to remember our loved one and our need to celebrate.

Consider how Jesus' mother might have felt as she opened her box of memories.

Mary cradled the wooden box in her arms. As she brushed her fingers across the lid's intricate carvings, she recalled the workshop in which it was crafted. Sawdust, shavings, and woodpiles lay on the floor beside a table strewn with hammers and saws. A man sanded a piece of wood while a small boy watched. Mary's eyes filled with tears. She recalled the twinkle in Jesus' eyes when he handed her the box as a gift. This was his first project as his father's helper.

Mary smiled and slowly opened the lid. Her heart began to pound in fear and anticipation of how she would respond to what was inside. No one else could understand this occasion's significance, but she knew she had to do this in spite of her fear.

Feeling anxious and afraid is something I should be used to, she thought, as she recalled fifty years earlier when an angel appeared, announced Jesus' birth, and told her not to be afraid.

With renewed confidence Mary opened the lid and gazed at the contents inside: a dried flower, a jagged rock, a piece of straw, a seed, and a piece of wood. Memories crashed onto the shore of her soul. She held the brittle flower in the palm of her hand and remembered the night Joseph had given it to her when they first married.

She chuckled as she held the jagged rock and recalled her bumpy ride to Bethlehem. *When the donkey stumbled on this rock, it nearly put me into labor. What a night to remember,* she thought. Then she held up the piece of straw from the stable where Jesus was born.

I almost forgot about this, she thought as she held the tiny seed. I didn't see much of Jesus after He left Nazareth because He was so busy traveling and teaching. But during one of His visits He told a story about a sower and some seed, so I put this seed in my box to remind me of the words He shared.

Mary's face grew solemn as she picked up the piece of wood. *Little did I know the significance that wood would play in my Son's life ... and in His death.* She recalled kneeling at the cross, watching her Son die, and the days of mourning that followed.

Mary looked at the empty box and smiled. *When I heard the tomb was empty and Jesus was alive again, I was so excited. God gave me hope that someday I'd see my Son again.*

She carefully placed the items back in the box and closed the lid. The experience had brought her a sad kind of pleasure; she was glad she had faced her fears.

Like Mary, remembering your loved one may lead you through the gate of thanksgiving. Celebrate your loved one today. Create a memory box and enclose items that represent something special about him or her. You may choose to open it often or only on special occasions. Your memory box can be a tool to help you embrace celebrating as part of your grief journey.

God, as I think about occasions that trigger memories of my loved one, I have mixed emotions. I'm afraid to open my box of memories, but I'm also eager to. I don't know how I'll respond. Be my guide and help me to know when I'm ready to have a day to remember. Replace my fear with hope. Help me to open the lid to my memories and to celebrate my loved one through laughter and tears. Thank You for the memories. Amen.

❧

MY PERSONAL JOURNEY

_____

_____

_____

_____

_____

_____

_____

_____

_____

_____

_____

_____

_____

_____

_____

_____

_____

Devotion 48

A TROPHY
TO REMEMBER

■ ■ ■

"Where, O death, is your victory? Where, O death, is your sting?" . . . But
thanks be to God! He gives us the victory through our Lord Jesus Christ.

1 CORINTHIANS 15:55, 57

"ON YOUR MARK. GET set. Go!" Racers thrust forward to capture the lead position. Partnering skill and technique with endurance, they press on to the finish line. The crowd cheers. How quickly the race ends, and then the victor steps forward, his face gleaming as the official awards him the championship trophy. That trophy stands as a monument of celebration, a symbol of his unyielding faith and perseverance to see his dream become reality.

Trophies give us a reason to celebrate and remember. When I dust my son Jake's trophies, I recall his first soccer season and his difficulty running in too-small shoes. His first swim team trophy reminds me of the summer when all his strokes looked the same. It also signifies a time just prior to his brother's death, a time when our family prepared to begin our grief journey.

Jake had prayed for years that God would give us a baby and was elated when his prayers were answered. Because we knew our baby was expected to die from fatal birth defects, we realized this outcome could destroy our son's faith in God. How could we overcome this obstacle of grief? How could we transform death into something victorious?

Then we remembered how Jake loved trophies. *That's it!* we thought.

A few days later Jake walked into my hospital room to hold his baby brother and say good-bye to him. His face was solemn and his eyes dimmed with disappointment as he touched his brother's fingers and toes. Jake knew he would never play catch with his little brother or kick a soccer ball to him.

"Jake, your brother has a gift for you."

I handed him a large trophy, decorated with a cross, a Bible, and praying hands.

Jake's eyes sparkled. "What does it say?" he asked as he pointed to the inscription.

With clarity and confidence I read, "To my big brother, Jake, because you prayed for me."

Celebrating and remembering our loved ones can bring healing to our souls. Whether the remembrance takes the form of a trophy, a recipe, a tradition, or a song, it doesn't matter. What matters is that we not ignore our loved one's memory and the opportunity we have to celebrate him or her. The process of remembering can help us in our journey through grief.

If you don't have memories about your loved one, create them. Start a celebration in his or her honor by giving an anonymous gift to a needy family on your loved one's birthday. Plant a tree or volunteer a day at a homeless shelter. Partner your skill and technique with perseverance and celebrate your loved one with a sense of victory.

Lord, I've been running in the race of grief, trying to cross the finish line. Sometimes I've stumbled, and it's been hard to get back up. But You've always been there. I want to press on and run with endurance and perseverance. Help me to celebrate my loved one's memories. Show me how I can create opportunities to honor him (her) that will help others. Be my victor and my strength today and help me to remember and celebrate the victories You have given me in my race through grief. Amen.

MY PERSONAL JOURNEY

REMEMBER, YET CELEBRATE!

■ ■ ■

Forgetting what is behind and straining toward what is ahead, I press on toward the goal to win the prize for which God has called me heavenward in Christ Jesus.

PHILIPPIANS 3:13B—14

Rejoice in the Lord always. I will say it again: Rejoice!

PHILIPPIANS 4:4

THE AROMA OF FRESH cut flowers filled the air while candles flickered and radiated a warm, welcome glow. People filed down the aisles as the organ played. Men clad in tuxedos and women in long gowns stood at the front of the room. The bridegroom stepped forward in eager anticipation. As his eyes scanned the pews, he saw four elderly aunts, uncles, cousins, and a sister, but his eyes misted with tears as he stared at the empty places where his parents should have been seated. *I wish they were here to celebrate with me today,* he thought.

Childhood memories flooded his mind ... being eight and having two parents ... then having only his mom. Then, at fifteen, his mom died too. He recalled passing his driver's test without them, moving away to college and enduring parents' weekends and the empty chairs at his high school and college graduations. Now his parents would miss his wedding day as well.

The bells chimed announcing his bride had arrived and his new life was about to begin. He turned from his past and looked to his future. In spite of the void in his life, he would celebrate this moment.

You may identify with my husband's story. You, too, may have celebrated special occasions with voids in your life. You have wished your loved one was sitting around the table or in the pew, sharing milestone moments.

Does time heal the pain and fill the void? Sometimes.

Is celebrating still possible in your journey through grief? Absolutely! But it's a choice you must make.

I've often wondered how the disciples felt when they shared their first Lord's Supper without Jesus. Seeing His empty chair at the table must have felt odd. They would have to celebrate without Him. For a moment the mood may have been solemn as they felt the void of their friend's companionship. They may have even reminisced about previous times with Jesus. Then the bread was passed and the cup. Jesus' words must have flooded their memories: "Do this in remembrance of me." They realized that He wanted them to carry on and press on to the future. He had asked them to celebrate without His physical presence.

We reach a point in our journey through grief in which we have to integrate our past into our future and celebrate our new identity and direction. My husband continues to teach me the importance of celebrating as we encounter meaningful times in our family's life without his parents.

Hours after our wedding, he told me he had one surprise stop to make before we left for the airport. My curiosity mounted as we drove through the gates of a wooded, estate-like setting. He took my hand and led me through a maze of stone markers. We stopped in front of a majestic pair, and he squeezed my hand and said, "I just wanted to remember them and include them on one of my happiest celebrations." Even though I never met Rich's parents, I know they were special. It's obvious every time I look at my husband.

It's okay to remember and to celebrate the joy of the moment.

God, I want to enjoy special occasions, but it's hard when I face an empty chair and realize my loved one can't share in my joy. My life has a void that others can't fill. Thank You for the memories I have of my loved one. Help me to turn from my past and face the future. Be my Lord, who communes with me in my pain and in my joy. Help me to journey on in my grief and celebrate. Amen.

MY PERSONAL JOURNEY

JOURNEY FROM WINTER TO SPRINGTIME

■ ■ ■

See! The winter is past; the rains are over and gone. Flowers appear on the earth; the season of singing has come, the cooing of doves is heard in our land.

SONG OF SONGS 2:11—12

SNOW DRIFTS. FREEZING TEMPERATURES. Howling winds. Frosted windowpanes. Gray skies. Icy driveways. Leafless trees.

Listening to the radio for school closures was a Midwest winter ritual for me during my childhood. When fierce blizzards hit, I could be homebound for days. Being confined was frustrating and depressing at times. As more snow piled up against our house, I wondered how I was going to dig out from the drifts.

But over time the snow melted, the temperatures climbed, rays of sunshine gleamed, and stalks of green grass poked through the ground. Springtime always ushered in new hopes, new life, and new looks. To shed layers of winter wool and sport a cheery new wardrobe was uplifting.

As we journey through grief, we may experience winter, when inner "frosting" occurs. We become resentful and frustrated by the storms of our circumstance. Blizzards of sadness blow through. We are snowed in, confined in our depression and hopeless of ever digging out.

When we feel this inner coldness, we need to remember how God renews the earth from the deadness of winter with springtime's vibrant beauty. Just as God created sunshine to melt the ice and snow, so His love's sunshine melts the frost of our pain and grief.

Maybe today is the day to shed your winter wardrobe of grief and clothe yourself with a new spring look of hope and life. As you embrace the springtime, you may sense a new identity budding, possibilities blooming, and a renewed attitude poking up through the soil of your soul. Though you still miss your loved one, you feel alive again.

The winter of your grieving has passed, and you've survived it. It's time to celebrate springtime. Embrace it. Thank God. Live. Hope. Grow. Renew your mind and heart in the sunshine of God's love.

God, thank You for being with me through the winter of my grieving. As my sunshine, defrost my frozen heart and attitude. Thank You that You will bring springtime to my soul with Your love. Renew my life and clothe me with hope. Enable me to embrace the new opportunities and possibilities that You reveal to me today. Help me to celebrate that winter will pass and to embrace my journey to springtime. Amen.

MY PERSONAL JOURNEY

_____

_____

_____

_____

_____

_____

_____

_____

YOUR JOURNEY THROUGH RELATING

Relating: *to tell, to show, to establish a logical or casual connection between, to connect with.*

■ ■ ■

God whispers to us in our pleasures, speaks in our conscience, but shouts in our pains: it is His megaphone to arouse a deaf world.

C. S. LEWIS

Grief can cause us to relate differently to God, ourselves, and others. We may look the same, but we are forever changed and must learn to communicate and connect in new ways. We speak a new tongue: the language of loss.

KATHE WUNNENBERG

Empathy is your pain in my heart.

AUTHOR UNKNOWN

LANDSCAPING LOSS
INTO YOUR LIFE

∎ ∎ ∎

Even the wilderness and desert will rejoice in those days; the desert will blos-
som with flowers. Yes, there will be an abundance of flowers and singing and
joy! The deserts will become as green as the Lebanon mountains, as lovely as
Mount Carmel's pastures and Sharon's meadows; for the Lord will display his
glory there, the excellency of our God.

ISAIAH 35:1–2, TLB

I WENT TO SEE Carol the day after her husband died. When she came to
the door, I greeted her with a box of tissues and a hug. Then I spent time
listening to her recall her final hours with Bill. His sudden death had
uprooted her sense of identity. Yesterday she was his business partner
and wife. Today, she was the business's sole owner and a widow. How
could she relate to this new identity?

I knew nothing would dissolve Carol's pain, but I wanted to give her
words of hope. "Carol, you're in the process of landscaping."

She looked puzzled yet intrigued.

"Your loss is like a tree that's been chopped down in your backyard,"
I explained. Ironically, I had just read this illustration in the book *A Grace
Disguised*, and I was now relating it to Carol in my own words. "All that
remains is a brown, ugly stump. That stump is a constant reminder of the
beautiful tree you've lost. Each time you look out the window, all you can
see is that stump. Eventually, you will decide to do something about the
stump. Instead of getting rid of it, you may decide to landscape around it.
You might plant some shrubs, flowers, and other trees. In time you may
even decide to put a walkway leading up to it with a couple of benches to
sit on. The stump will always remind you of the beautiful tree you lost, but

someday it will be surrounded by a beautiful garden. Although your sorrow will remain, you'll have the opportunity to create a landscape around it so that what was once ugly will be part of a larger, lovely whole."

Carol nodded and squeezed my hand.

A few days later I received a call from Carol. "Kathe, you're never going to believe this. A pastor working as a part-time tree-trimmer came to my door. One of our large trees was too close to the house and needed to be cut down, and I began to tell him the stump story. He left but came back a few minutes later and said, 'Carol, the Lord told me to leave you a tree stump so that's what I'm going to do.' I'm looking at my stump right now. I guess I'll need to start landscaping around it!"

Sooner or later we all suffer loss. It may be packaged in little doses or big ones, suddenly or over time, privately or in a public setting. Loss is as much a part of everyday life as birth. Our experience of loss is not the defining moment that transforms us but how we respond to it. The way we relate to that loss will largely determine the direction, the quality, and the impact of our lives.

Loss is a part of who I am. It's an integral part of my identity. I cringe when people ask me, "Are you over it yet?" I'll never "get over" losing my children. Instead, we must learn to integrate loss into our lives, to relate to it despite our feelings of uncertainty and inadequacy. Only God is able to guide us on this quest to learn simply to be who we are . . . widowed, childless, parentless, sisterless, friendless. Life can still be good, just different than it was before.

Lord, part of my life has been cut down. My stump of loss reminds me of my loved one and who I once was but am no longer. Who am I now? Where do I go from here? Help me to sort out who I am, to reconsider my priorities, and to determine new directions. You are the Master Gardener. Transform my stump into a setting that is lush and beautiful. Show me how to relate to loss and to landscape it into my life in a way that glorifies You. Amen.

My Personal Journey

Devotion 52

GRIEF MENTOR

■ ■ ■

And the things you have heard me say in the presence of many witnesses
entrust to reliable men who will also be qualified to teach others.

2 TIMOTHY 2:2

NAOMI ROCKED BACK AND forth, trying to find a way to contain her grief. She wondered why she had to endure first the loss of her husband and now her two sons. Why had the Lord taken them? What should she do next?

Then she saw her daughter-in-law's tearstained face. Naomi cradled Ruth in her arms and wept with her, stroking her hair and wiping her tears.

Naomi recalled the first time her son had brought Ruth home. Naomi had dreamed of a daughter-in-law from her own country, but the famine had forced her family to move to Moab. Then her worst fears came to pass when her son announced he would marry Ruth, a woman of a different faith. Yet, over the years Naomi had grown to love Ruth. Naomi had taught her how to cook her son's favorite foods, to sew, and to mend clothing. Naomi had talked openly about the Lord and even had prayed when Ruth was present.

Now, sharing Ruth's pain triggered the memory of Ruth's husband's death. She relived the hurtful words many had spoken and her longing for someone to comfort her and relate to her pain. Naomi had learned the language of loss and now knew how to respond to Ruth. With her experience, Naomi could teach her daughter-in-law about grief and being a widow. She could be Ruth's grief mentor.

Mentoring is as old as civilization. This natural, relational process allows the wiser, more experienced person to pass on insights to others. The Bible is rich with mentoring examples: Moses and Joshua, Elijah and Elisha, Paul and Timothy, and Naomi and Ruth.

Webster's Dictionary defines mentor as a "trusted counselor and guide," but a mentor is much more. Mentors are like pathfinders who have scaled the mountain we intend to climb. They call down from farther up the mountain and encourage us to keep climbing. They warn us to watch the rocks, stay on the path, and not give up. They enlarge our perceptions and give us the confidence that, like them, we can overcome obstacles and achieve our dreams. Mentors help us to open and close the important chapters in our lives.

That's how God used Dottie in my life — to mentor me through my grief. Several years earlier she had lost a daughter with the same rare birth defect as my son. I had watched her endure the emotional pain of carrying a child destined to die and her grief journey through the years. Although we didn't communicate regularly, I always felt a kindred spirit with her, and when I discovered I was to lose my child in the same way she had lost hers, I knew I could scale my mountain of grief because she had. She was my mentor farther up the mountain, who gave me the courage to press on.

Being a grief mentor isn't a role I would have chosen, but God has enabled me to gain insights to share with others and to give them hope. God is the divine Connector who knows whom we need, when we need them, and where they are. All we need to do is ask Him to connect us with those who can mentor us through grief — or whom we can mentor when we have journeyed farther down the path.

Grief mentoring may consist of meeting with someone once, regular phone conversations, or a lifelong relationship. You and the other person need to agree on the purpose, expectations, and life cycle of the relationship.

Passing on what we know may require us to initiate the relationship. Many long for encouragement in their grief journey but are afraid to voice their need. We may have to approach a person and let him or her know we care by asking questions and taking the first steps to offer encouragement.

If others were to look to you as a grief mentor, what would you want them to see in you? What insights could you pass on that would give hope to others?

When I look back at each chapter in my life, I can name people whom God used in mentoring roles. Most had "been there, done that." They shared their insights, expertise, and knowledge with me in person or from afar. Some were there through timely cards and brief phone conversations. Others invested long hours in person. Some of my mentors were people I've never met but know by watching them from afar or from reading about their lives — like Ruth and Naomi. God has used people of all ages to give me timely insights, hope, and courage to press on.

What about you? Who are the people who have influenced you through your grief journey or whose life you have influenced? Thank God and thank them!

God, You are the divine Connector. You know exactly whom I need in my relational network to help me scale my mountain of grief. You also know who needs me to give them insight and encouragement. Thank You that I am not alone in my journey and that there are those who are willing to walk with me for a season. Show me who they are and give me the courage to ask them to help me. Open my eyes to the needs of others and use me to comfort them as well. Amen.

❧

MY PERSONAL JOURNEY

_____

_____

_____

My Personal Journey

CONNECTING THROUGH LOSS

—■ ■ ■————————————————

No one has ever seen God; but if we love one another, God lives in us and his love is made complete in us.

1 JOHN 4:12

REALITY HIT WHEN I saw the "For Sale" sign posted in the yard next door. Thirteen years of being neighbors with Theresa would soon come to an end. Through laughter and tears I recalled the life experiences we had shared: landscaping, garage sales, starting a home-based business, progressive dinner parties, coping with living apart from family, becoming parents, new careers, divorce, and death.

God knew that Theresa was someone I needed during that season in my life. She had understood how it felt to be childless and to endure Mother's Day with empty arms. When I labored through the adoption process, she was my cheerleader, ready to share her insights from adopting two children and being available to be our full-time baby-sitter. It's hard to find neighbors like that.

In preparation for our new neighbors, we made a "neighbor wish list" and began to pray for our neighbors-to-be.

While waiting on God's answer, we experienced the fatal prognosis of our baby and our son's birth and death. Just weeks after his funeral, we saw a family walk out of the house next door. Could this be they? We smiled and waved. They smiled and waved back. "Are you interested in the house?" we asked. They nodded and walked closer.

We told them that the best part of buying the house was to have us as neighbors! We all laughed. Then I noticed their two-year-old daughter and a small white bundle in the woman's arms. "How old is your baby?" I asked.

"Three months," she replied.

What a coincidence, I thought. *Our baby would be two months old.*

A few days later we saw the "Sold" sign. The young family we met would be our new neighbors. My new neighbor, Stephanie, was just the person I needed for this season of my life. She had experienced the death of an infant son a year earlier. His name was Jacob, our living son's name.

God knew exactly what He was doing by connecting our lives. He gave me much more than I had prayed for. He hand-selected a neighbor who understood my joy, my sorrow, and my journey through grief.

God, I'm beginning to realize that lots of people speak the language of loss; I'm not alone in my journey through grief. Others can relate to some of the challenges I face without my loved one. Thank You for being Jehovah Jireh, the God who provides, and for providing people to comfort me. In turn, use me to reach out to comfort others. Reveal to me a person I can encourage today. Amen.

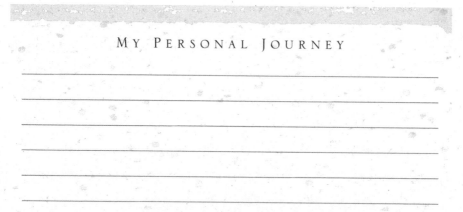

MY PERSONAL JOURNEY

My Personal Journey

Devotion 54

EXPECT THE UNEXPECTED

■ ■ ■

Many are the plans in a man's heart, but it is the LORD's purpose that prevails.

PROVERBS 19:21

GRABBING MY LUGGAGE, I hurried through the airport. As I approached my gate, I noticed a "flight delayed" sign posted.

I can't believe it! What will I do for two hours? I grumbled. I edged my way to the only vacant seat in a crowded corner and reluctantly sat down across from a young woman with a new baby. She looked sad, and I noticed she wasn't wearing a wedding ring.

Instinctively I knew she needed a friend, so I started a conversation with her. As I listened, her tearful story unraveled. A dam seemed to break, and all her hurts and fears came rushing out . . . abuse, broken relationships, betrayal, abandonment, and death.

Feelings of inadequacy gripped me. Although I could relate to some of her challenges, I didn't view myself as an authority. I considered dashing to the rest room or suggesting she seek professional help, but then it occurred to me that my flight delay and this meeting were no coincidence. Maybe part of the reason God had brought me through my own grief was to help this young woman.

Help me say the right thing, God, I prayed silently.

"I'm sorry you are hurting," I said as I handed her a tissue. "Although I don't know exactly how you feel, I can relate to some of your hurts."

"How did you cope?" she asked.

For the remaining minutes before our flight departed I shared how God's unconditional, steadfast relationship had given me hope and was available to her too.

Unplanned interruptions may be disguised as sleepless nights, a long line in a store, a flat tire, or a delayed flight. I used to dread change and the unknown, but God has given me a new attitude, an expectant heart for the opportunities that await me. I expect the unexpected now, and I'm not surprised when my schedule changes. I find myself chuckling and saying, "Okay, God, what do You want me to learn through this and whom do You want me to relate to?" I don't want to miss an opportunity to serve because the delay is inconvenient or because it seems risky to reach out to someone.

The next time a change in your plans occurs, don't miss the opportunity for a divine appointment!

Lord, thanks for planning interruptions in my life and providing opportunities for me to relate to others in my journey through grief. Forgive me for not always having a ready, positive attitude and for missing divine appointments to bring hope and healing to others. Help me to expect the unexpected and be ready to adjust my schedule to Yours. I give You permission to change my plans and to use me to help others. Be my counselor and guide today and show me whom You want me to relate to. Amen.

MY PERSONAL JOURNEY

_____

_____

_____

_____

MY PERSONAL JOURNEY

_____

_____

_____

_____

_____

_____

_____

_____

_____

_____

_____

_____

_____

_____

_____

_____

_____

_____

_____

_____

_____

_____

_____

JOURNEY TO THE POND OF RELATING

■ ■ ■

*Praise be to the God and Father of our Lord Jesus Christ, the Father of com-
passion and the God of all comfort, who comforts us in all our troubles, so
that we can comfort those in any trouble with the comfort we ourselves have
received from God.*

2 CORINTHIANS 1:3–4

"WHISPERING PINES." WHEN GRANNIE and I saw the sign on the tree,
we knew we had almost reached our destination. Just a few more steps
through the woods, and then we saw it . . . the pond. The round body of
brownish-green water in the middle of the forest was home to a multitude of creatures. A frog plopped into the water. A dragonfly lit on the
floating lily pad. Deer tracks lined the bank. Tadpoles, turtles, fish, and
crayfish lived beneath the surface.

I picked up two rocks and clicked them together. I paused, then did
it again. The frog replied and bellowed out a deep, "Croak. Croak.
Croak."

Grannie motioned for me to sit on the tree stump next to hers. We
watched the sun's mid-morning rays dance across the water's surface
and shared a sandwich and a candy bar.

Then Grannie picked up a rock and hurled it through the air to the
center of the pond. Plop! Waves rippled in concentric circles to the
pond's edge. First one circle, then another, then another. I was amazed
to think that such a small object could make such a difference.

Sooner or later our journey through grief will take us to the Pond of
Relating. We may wander through the wilderness for awhile until we see

the road sign that points the way. Then we'll realize that our longtime companions — solitude and sadness — have been with us long enough. Now is the time to allow the sunlight to dance across our souls and for us to be with others.

After being with solitude and sadness for so long, we doubt that our loss can make a difference to anyone else. Then a woman motions for us to sit by her. We feel at ease and begin to share about our journey through grief and what we've learned. She looks encouraged, and we discover she has just lost someone too.

Then a man motions for her to sit by him. She does, and we listen as she passes on our insights to him. We watch as the cycle continues. One person, then another, then another. As we hurl the rock of our loss into the center of the pond of relationships, we see the ripple effects that relating our loss to others can have.

If you're not convinced that you and your loss can have an eternal effect in other's lives, consider Jesus. He invested Himself in twelve men's lives . . . who invested in others . . . who invested in others . . . who invested in others. The ripple effect of His life changed the world and still does today, even though He is gone physically.

How have others made a ripple effect in your life? How has God already used the loss of your loved one to impact others' lives? How can you allow Him to use you to pass on what you know?

Go ahead. Journey to the Pond of Relating. Throw in your stone of loss and watch the ripple effect!

God, show me if this is the time You want me to help others. Thank You for the people who have made a difference in my life. I don't want my loss to be stagnant. Instead, reveal to me how my loved one's life already has touched others. Show me how I can encourage fellow grievers. Be the Rock in my loss. Make an eternal ripple effect through me on others. Amen.

MY PERSONAL JOURNEY

Section 12 Living

YOUR JOURNEY
TO LIVING

Living: *to show life, conduct, or manner of life;
active; functioning; the power to grow.*

■ ■ ■

My life was suddenly divided into before and after, and
there was no going back to before. But then I realized I
had a choice to live the after. I had to decide.

BRENDA NEAL, *A TIME TO MOURN, A TIME TO DANCE*

I wish for you the joy of holding life with an open hand.
Just let go of all the stuff you've had to worry about
and hang on and protect. . . . It isn't what you have that
predetermines your strength now or in the future. It is
what you are willing to let go of that is the ultimate test.

BOB BENSON, *SEE YOU AT THE HOUSE*

He belongs to you, but more than that, He longs to be
in you, living and ruling in you, as the head lives and
rules the body. He wants His breath to be in your
breath, His heart in your heart, and His soul in your
soul, so that you may indeed, "Glorify God and bear
Him in your body, that the life of Jesus may be manifest
in you."

JEAN EUDES

Devotion 56

JOURNEY TO THE
LIGHTHOUSE OF LIVING

■ ■ ■

*I am the light of the world. Whoever follows me will never walk in darkness,
but will have the light of life.*

JOHN 8:12B

OCEAN WAVES CRASH AGAINST the shore as fog and darkness move in.
Hidden beneath the water's surface lies a minefield of rocks waiting for
the unsuspecting ship that sails too close to the coastline. Then, just as
the seafarers near the rocks, a beacon of light pierces through the foggy
night as if to say, "Danger, danger." The sailors respond to the warning
and steer away. The lighthouse has fulfilled its purpose.

Lighthouses have been around since the seventh century and usually
are constructed at strategic or isolated points on a coastline. They project light at night and serve as a marker by day to safely guide ships sailing in coastal waters. As lighthouses illuminate the darkness, guide
through danger and destruction, and point the way to living, they serve
as beacons of hope.

At times in our grief journey, we experience the darkness and fog of
our loss, and we near destruction. Other times, we may realize that loss
has enlarged our lives, and we can be beacons of hope to others.

Like a lighthouse, we may stand alone in the darkness and fog.
Hidden rocks of discouragement, hopelessness, and bitterness lie in wait
of unsuspecting people. Lives will be lost unless someone lights the way.
"Shine through us to warn others and to guide them safely through," we

cry out to God. In this way, we become lighthouses to everyone we meet, proclaiming God's hope and life. Then we realize that God has enlarged our souls through loss and allowed us to embrace living again.

When Jesus said, "I am the light of the world. Whoever follows me will never walk in darkness, but will have the light of life," He was claiming to be the light by which truth and falsehood are distinguished. Light reveals reality and destroys the deception and illusion that darkness brings. Jesus' light brings God's presence, protection, and guidance into our lives. He becomes our lighthouse and illuminates our way.

Look around. A world full of people need to be warned and guided from death to life. These people need God's presence, protection, and guidance. Your journey through grief has led you this far so you can be a beacon of hope and a lighthouse for the living. Will you be Christ's light today to people in need? Will you allow God to use your experience of loss to radiate hope to others? Embrace living and be a lighthouse, just as God has been for you.

God, thank You for being the light of the world and the light of life. You are my lighthouse, who protects and guides me in my journey through grief. You point the way to living. Illuminate my life with Your truth. Help me to be a beacon of hope to others who need encouragement or need to know You. Show me who is destined to be destroyed and provide opportunities for me to be a lighthouse to guide them to living. Amen.

MY PERSONAL JOURNEY

_____

_____

_____

My Personal Journey

Devotion 57

LIVING WITH NEW ROLES
AND EXPECTATIONS

■ ■ ■

Endure hardship with us like a good soldier of Christ Jesus. No one serving as a soldier gets involved in civilian affairs — he wants to please his commanding officer.

2 TIMOTHY 2:3—4

WHILE PACKING FOR A business trip, Bob noticed piles of clothes, books, and workshop materials scattered all over the floor and wondered how everything was going to fit in the suitcase. The last time he had attempted this feat, he had destroyed his baggage. So reluctantly, he decided to leave a few things behind.

Later, during his flight, he realized that his luggage was similar to his life, bulging with expectations and about to burst with more opportunities than any one person should be asked to carry. *But I'm not doing that much,* he rationalized.

He made a list to ease his conscience. To his amazement, he discovered twenty-seven roles that he was juggling. Since his wife's death, he had comforted himself by making busyness his constant companion. Maybe it helped to mask his pain or it distracted him from feeling the void. Whatever the reason, he knew he needed to lighten his load, evaluate his expectations, and redefine his roles during this season of his journey.

Bob began by asking himself, What is my motive for doing what I do — is it my expectations, others' expectations, or God's expectations?

After sifting each of his roles through the grid of this question, he discovered some roles (being a child of God, a dad, and a son, and caring for himself) only he could fulfill. Many roles, though meaningful and good, could be delegated or deleted during the healing season of his grief journey.

Bob realized that he was driven to roles and activities he felt he could control. He wondered if his underlying motive was because he couldn't control his loved one's death. Bob's personal expectations were unrealistic, and he needed to relinquish many of his roles. He needed to trust God to help him put a stop to his busyness and learn to adjust to the roles He had for him during his grief journey.

It occurred to Bob that experiencing life to the fullest is like using a map. If the map he used was accurate, he could know with certainty where he was, where he needed to go, and how he could get there. If it was false, he would be overwhelmed, misguided, and lost.

Since he was afraid to trust himself and others to guide him, he sought a more reliable map to lead him in his grief journey to living — God's Word. He began to follow the route the Bible prescribed. He prayed more, studied the Bible, listened to God without talking, meditated on the Word, and evaluated his motives based on God's expectations.

As Bob sought truth, he was reminded that Jesus juggled the roles of mentor, teacher, healer, friend, evangelist, carpenter, child of God, and fellow griever. He wondered if Jesus ever felt overwhelmed or disappointed. Because Jesus' motives were pure and His decision-making was rooted in God's expectations, Bob knew Jesus had chosen to live the right roles. Jesus had set boundaries and priorities in spite of others' expectations. He had made time with God and time for rest and restoration. He had mastered living with expectations that pulled Him in many directions and with a variety of ever-changing roles.

What about you? Is your life bulging with roles and expectations? Is it about to burst? Is busyness a distraction from your grief? Are you motivated by your expectations, others' expectations, or God's expectations?

Maybe you need to evaluate, relinquish unrealistic expectations, and map out a strategy rooted in truth so that you can please God and live the way He intended you to. Trust me, lightening your load and living with God's expectations is a map worth following.

*God, sometimes I become overwhelmed with all the roles and expecta-
tions I juggle. Then I become scared to slow down and let go because I'll feel
the pain and void in my life from my loss. The role I once filled is no longer
a part of who I am, and that makes me feel lost. Help me evaluate my
motives, relinquish inappropriate or unnecessary roles, and map out a
strategy based in Your expectations. Guide me through this part of my
journey through grief and help me to adjust to new roles. Amen.*

MY PERSONAL JOURNEY

_____

_____

_____

_____

_____

_____

_____

_____

_____

_____

_____

_____

_____

_____

_____

BEING THANKFUL
IS IN ORDER

Give thanks in all circumstances, for this is God's will for you in Christ Jesus.

1 THESSALONIANS 5:18

I WAS PLEASANTLY SURPRISED when friends provided us with a much-needed family getaway to a bed-and-breakfast in Flagstaff, Arizona, after the loss of our son. The thought of cool temperatures, pine trees, no phones, and no schedules invigorated me. I hadn't felt that way in a long time; this was just the restoration my soul needed. I could see myself sweater-clad, sipping coffee, book in hand, nestled in a rocking chair on the inn's turn-of-the-century front porch. I envisioned time for laughter, naps, family walks, playing games, and meaningful conversations.

No sooner had we checked into our nostalgic suite than I was jolted by reality. "Kath, where's the television?" My husband's tone of voice told me he wasn't prepared to hear my response.

"This is a place to relax. There is no television," I announced.

"No television? You know that's how I unwind."

This was going to be a long weekend after all.

Relief engulfed me when a train whistle from the nearby depot sounded and Jake asked, "Mom, can we go see the trains now?"

I was determined to have a great time. But by midnight we realized that the hourly train whistles were a fixture of this place. By 2:00 A.M. we were singing along to the music blaring through the wall. Our

thumps on the wall apparently had been ignored or unheard by the celebrating guests. By 3:00 A.M. my knock on the neighbors' door and
pleading with them worked, and we were finally able to sleep.

The seven o'clock train ended our slumber. Rich strode into the
bathroom to take his shower, but moments later he bellowed, "There's
no water!"

I sought immediate counsel from the innkeepers. They told me the
city had failed to notify them about work on the water main. They apol-
ogized for the inconvenience. When I reentered our room with this
news, I took one look at Rich's face (and hair) and knew I shouldn't sug-
gest breakfast in the inn's formal dining room. Instead, I encouraged
Rich to wear a hat, and we went out.

The hour-long wait at the restaurant fueled our frustration, and by
the time we were seated at a table, I'm embarrassed to admit the three
of us were barely speaking to one another.

"Mom, I need to go to the bathroom," Jake whined.

"It's your turn, Rich!" I snapped.

Alone at the table, I sipped my coffee and surveyed my dashed
expectations for this weekend, only to be interrupted by Rich and Jake's
premature return.

Rich sighed. "You're not going to be believe this. The bathroom is out
of order!"

We erupted in a trio of laughter. During breakfast we made amends
to God and to each other. After we released our expectations, we were
able to enjoy the rest of our time together, determined to be thankful —
no matter what!

God taught me a valuable lesson that weekend. Even when my
expectations or circumstances are "out of order," a thankful response is
"in order." And that applies not only to bed-and-breakfast accommodations but also to the grieving process. When we expect to be farther
along in the process than we are, when our progress seems slow, or
when we are jolted back to an earlier stage we thought we were through

with, our expectations may be out of order. But if we can find within ourselves the wherewithal to be thankful for how far we've come, for how faithful God has been to us, for the progress we know the Lord will enable us to make, then our response will be "in order."

What expectations have caused you to feel frustrated with your grief journey? As you've tried to deal with your loss, what circumstances have caught you by surprise and left you feeling confused and hurt? Release your expectations and embrace thankfulness — it will make the journey so much easier.

God, I admit that often my expectations are out of order, especially when it comes to grief. Forgive me for the times I'm too hard on myself and others. Help me to give thanks in all circumstances and to embrace living from Your perspective. Thank You for laughter, friends, family, time away, Your Word, and even for the disappointments You have enabled me to endure. Remind me that You are in control of my living and that being thankful in all circumstances is "in order." Amen.

MY PERSONAL JOURNEY

_____

_____

_____

_____

_____

_____

_____

_____

My Personal Journey

Devotion 59

LIVING BEYOND
THE "NO"

■ ■ ■

For nothing is impossible with God.

LUKE 1:37

THE INNKEEPER WHO GAVE Mary and Joseph a stable to stay in should be a model for us as we celebrate important seasons like Christmas without our loved one. That's because the innkeeper had the ability to think and live beyond the "no." "No room in the inn" could easily have been his complete conversation with the visiting strangers who came to his door. But he didn't let perceived limitations stop him. Instead, he thought of other options.

In contrast, many of us who grieve are quick to say "no way" to people and circumstances. Too often we limit God's possibilities. When faced with a seemingly impossible circumstance, we convince ourselves there is no hope, no chance, no way!

What is the circumstance on your "no way" list?

My list is probably similar to yours. It's long. It contains names of insensitive people who will never understand my loss and people who care but won't stop giving advice and answers to why God allowed my loss. It includes people whom I think will never have a relationship with God, and others who are proud and will never see the need to change or learn humility. My list includes expectations that others have of me that I can't fulfill and my inability to cope with my new identity since my loss.

The names and circumstances on my list and yours share a common theme . . . a need for hope, a need for someone bigger than the circumstance, a need to think and live beyond the "no."

Christmas is God's reminder that He has heard our cry and responded. Because of sin, humankind was eternally separated from God. No hope. No chance. No way! But God thought beyond the "no."

He provided a way for us to have a relationship with Him and eternal life through the birth and death of His Son, Jesus. Celebrating Jesus' birth at Christmas and His death and resurrection at Easter remind us that the door of healing and salvation is open wide to all who will receive Him.

Don't allow your grief to limit God's possibilities in your life or in other's lives. Give Him your "no way" list today. Ask God to help you see beyond your circumstance and to change your "no way" thinking. It's time to journey on and to live beyond the "no."

God, thank You for being Emmanuel, God with us. Thank You for Christmas and for Easter and for thinking beyond the "no." Please forgive me for my "no way" thinking. Help me to trust You and to have Your perspective. Your Word says that with You nothing is impossible. Be my hope. Help me to see new possibilities and live beyond the "no." Amen.

MY PERSONAL JOURNEY

_____

_____

_____

_____

My Personal Journey

LIVING IN THE
FATHER'S ARMS

■ ■ ■

The eternal God is your refuge, and underneath are the everlasting arms.

DEUTERONOMY 33:27

WHEN I WAS A child, my dad used to take me with him in his gas truck to make deliveries to farmers in the country. I barely could see over the dashboard, so Dad sat me on a gallon oilcan. When we arrived at our delivery destination, I loved to help him pump the gas into the immense tanks. My ritual was to perch atop the back of the gas truck and watch him climb up and down the ladder. I felt safe and secure until the tank was full and I needed to get down. Because I was afraid of heights, fear overshadowed me. It felt too risky to jump.

My dad must have sensed my fear because he always came to my rescue. With a confident smile and outstretched arms, he would coax me to jump. Trembling with fear, I stood at the edge and looked into my dad's eyes. "Jump, I'll catch you," he would repeat.

Somehow I knew I could trust him. I took a deep breath, closed my eyes, and jumped. How comforting to feel his arms wrapped tightly around me! I was safe in my daddy's arms.

We reach a point in our journey through grief where we want to enjoy life's scenery, but we're "viewing impaired" and can't see above the dashboard of our loss. That's when we may receive an unexpected word of encouragement or an act of kindness from others who give us a lift.

They may even try to coax us back into the circle of involvement. We want to embrace living, but we're afraid to jump. Fear, guilt, and uncertainty hold us back.

God understands. His Word soothes our anxious hearts. His Spirit calms our fears. If we open our eyes to His presence, we may even sense Him standing there, smiling with outstretched arms. "Jump into living," He says. "I'll catch you." Will you trust Him? Will you jump?

As you reflect on your journey through grief, remember He is with you through your fog of denial and your volcano of anger. He helps you wander through the Wilderness of Why. He walks with you in the marketplace of bargaining, weeps with you through the flash flood of tears, and gives you courage in the fire of surrender. When you journey to the aisle of acceptance, He offers a tissue and a candle. He is your Mountain Mover as you praise your way through pain and your Transformer in your cocoon of being. He rejoices with you as you celebrate your framed memories and connects with you as you journey to the Pond of Relating. Why would He leave you now as you get ready to jump into the journey of living? He is the Way, the Truth, and the Life. You can trust Him on this part of your journey through grief too. He's waiting to catch you. Go ahead, jump!

Living in the Father's arms is the best place to be now and for all eternity. Are you certain that you will live with Him in heaven, where death, pain, tears, and sorrow no longer exist? Make sure of that today. Choose living.

> *Everlasting Father, thank You for being with me on my journey through grief. Your light and companionship comfort me. I'm ready to journey on to embrace living, but I'm anxious and afraid. Replace my fear with faith and my trembling with trust. Help me to jump into Your arms. I need You in my life right now. I believe that You are the Way, the Truth, and the Life and that You stretched out Your arms on the cross and died for me. You overcame death, rose again, and are preparing a place for me to live eternally with You. I look forward to being in heaven with You. Today, I commit to live in Your arms forever. Amen.*

MY PERSONAL JOURNEY

SUGGESTED RESOURCES

Books

Baker, Don. *Pain's Hidden Purpose.* Portland: Multnomah, 1984.

Cloninger, Claire. *Postcards for People Who Hurt.* Dallas: Word, 1995.

DeYmaz, Linda. *Mommy, Please Don't Cry.* Gresham, Oregon: Vision, 1996.

Dobson, James. *When God Doesn't Make Sense.* Wheaton, Illinois: Tyndale, 1993.

Erbe, Margie. *Danny, I Miss You So.* Self-published, 1995. (P.O. Box 39364, Phoenix, AZ 85069.)

Fitzgerald, Helen. *The Mourning Handbook: The Most Comprehensive Resource for Practical and Compassionate Advice on Coping with All Aspects of Death and Dying.* New York: Simon and Schuster, 1994.

Fitzpatrick, Carol. *A Time to Grieve.* Uhrichsville, Ohio: Barbour, 1995.

Graham, Billy. *Facing Death: And the Life After.* Minneapolis: Grason, 1987.

Hayford, Jack. *I'll Hold You in Heaven.* Ventura, California: Regal, 1986.

Huntley, Theresa. *Helping Children Grieve: When Someone You Love Dies.* Minneapolis: Augsburg, 1991.

Kinnaman, Gary. *My Companion Through Grief.* Ann Arbor: Servant, 1996.

Lewis, C. S. *A Grief Observed.* San Francisco: Harper & Row, reprinted 1989.

Miles, Margaret Shandor. *The Grief of a Parent When a Child Dies.* Oak Brook, Illinois: Compassionate Friends, 1978.

Mitsch, Raymond, and Lynn Brookside. *Grieving the Loss of Someone You Love.* Ann Arbor: Servant, 1993.

Myers, Ruth. *31 Days of Praise.* Sisters, Oregon: Multnomah, 1994.

Pink, Michael and Brenda. *Grace for Grief.* Grand Rapids: World, 1995.

Rank, Maureen. *Free to Grieve.* Minneapolis: Bethany, 1985.

Sittser, Gerald. *A Grace Disguised.* Grand Rapids: Zondervan, 1996.

Smith, Hannah Whitall. *The God of All Comfort.* Chicago: Moody, 1956.

Vredevelot, Pam. *Empty Arms.* Sisters, Oregon: Multnomah, 1984.

Westberg, Granger. *Good Grief.* Philadelphia: Fortress, 1972.

Wunnenberg, Kathe. *Grieving the Child I Never Knew*. Grand Rapids: Zondervan, forthcoming in 2000.

Yancey, Philip. *Where Is God When It Hurts?* Grand Rapids: Zondervan, 1977.

Magazine

Bereavement Magazine. Colorado Springs, Colorado. (719) 266–0006.

Music

Aaron Jeoffrey. "After the Rain, Beyond," from *After The Rain*, Star Song, 1996.

Beyond the Blue. "Reason for the Rain," from *Beyond the Blue*, Word, 1996.

Becker, Margaret. "I Will Be with You," from *Soul*, Sparrow, 1993.

Brunsting, Karen. *From Tragedy to Triumph — The Concert*, self-published, 616–652–6349.

Chapman, Steven Curtis. "With Hope," from *Speechless*, Sparrow, 1999

Keaggy, Cheri. "My Faith Will Stay, Keep on Shinin', Lay It Down," from *My Faith Will Stay*, Sparrow, 1996.

Kenoly, Ron. "Mourning into Dancing," from *Lift Him Up*, Hosanna Music, 1992.

Krippayne, Scott. "Every Single Tear," from *Bright Star Blue Sky*, Spring Hill Records, 1999.

Lewis, Crystal. "Beauty for Ashes," from *Beauty for Ashes*, Myrrh Records, 1996.

Meece, David. "Brokenness, Inside Out," from *Once in a Lifetime*, Star Song, 1993.

Moore, Kim. "God Makes No Mistakes," from *Beyond Redemption*, Heart's Desire Music, 1996.

Paris, Twila. "Hold on, I Am Not Afraid Anymore, I Will Listen," from *Where I Stand*, Sparrow, 1996.

———. "A Visitor from Heaven," from *Beyond a Dream*, Sparrow, 1993.

Point of Grace. "Jesus Will Still Be There," from *Point of Grace*, Word, 1993.

Thum, Pam. "Feel the Healing," from *Feel the Healing*, Benson, 1995.

Troccoli, Kathy. "Good-bye for Now," from *Corner of Eden*, Reunion Records, 1998.

Various artists. "Hold Me, Jesus," from *Awesome God — A Tribute to Rich Mullins*, Reunion Records, 1998.

SUPPORT ORGANIZATIONS

AARP Widowed Persons Service 202–434–2260
Washington, D.C.

American Association of Suicidology................ 202–237–2282
Washington, D.C.

The Compassionate Friends...................... 630–990–0010
Oak Brook, Illinois

MADD Mothers Against Drunk Driving........ 800–GET-MADD
Irving, Texas

National Hospice Organization 800–658–8898
Arlington, Virginia

Parents (family & friends) of Murdered Children 513–721–5683
Cincinnati, Ohio

RTS Bereavement Services (support and training
for professionals who work with the bereaved) 1–800–362–9567
Lutheran Hospital, LaCrosse, Wisconsin   ext. 4747

SIDS (Sudden Infant Death Syndrome) Alliance 800–221–7437
Baltimore, Maryland

For information on having Kathe Wunnenberg
speak to your group please contact:

Speak Up Speaker Services
1614 Edison Shores Pl.
Port Huron, MI 48060
1–888–870–7719
speakupinc@aol.com

Grieving the Child I Never Knew

Kathe Wunnenberg

"A tender and helpful book leading those who grieve over the death of an unborn child to the help they seek."

—ELISA MORGAN,
PRESIDENT AND CEO,
MOPS INTERNATIONAL

When the anticipation of your child's birth turns into the grief of miscarriage, tubal pregnancy, stillbirth, or early infant death, no words on earth can ease your loss. But there is strength and encouragement in the wisdom of others who have been there and found that God's comfort is real.

Having experienced three miscarriages and the death of an infant son, Kathe Wunnenberg knows the deep anguish of losing a child. *Grieving the Child I Never Knew* was born from her personal journey through sorrow. It is a wise and tender companion for mothers whose hearts have been broken—mothers like you whose dreams have been shattered and who wonder how to go on.

This devotional collection will help you grieve honestly and well. With seasoned insights and gentle questions, it invites you to present your hurts before God and to receive over time the healing that He alone can—and will—provide.

Each devotion includes:

- Scripture passage and prayer
- "Steps Toward Healing" questions
- Space for journaling
- Readings for holidays and special occasions

Hardcover: 978-O-310-22777-9

Pick up a copy today at your favorite bookstore!

Share Your Thoughts

With the Author: Your comments will be forwarded to the author when you send them to *zauthor@zondervan.com*.

With Zondervan: Submit your review of this book by writing to *zreview@zondervan.com*.

Free Online Resources at
www.zondervan.com

Zondervan AuthorTracker: Be notified whenever your favorite authors publish new books, go on tour, or post an update about what's happening in their lives at www.zondervan.com/authortracker.

Daily Bible Verses and Devotions: Enrich your life with daily Bible verses or devotions that help you start every morning focused on God. Visit www.zondervan.com/newsletters.

Free Email Publications: Sign up for newsletters on Christian living, academic resources, church ministry, fiction, children's resources, and more. Visit www.zondervan.com/newsletters.

Zondervan Bible Search: Find and compare Bible passages in a variety of translations at www.zondervanbiblesearch.com.

Other Benefits: Register yourself to receive online benefits like coupons and special offers, or to participate in research.

Z ZONDERVAN®

ZONDERVAN.com/
AUTHORTRACKER
follow your favorite authors